Harriet Hubbard.

A VOICE IN THE DARKNESS, A KNOCK AT THE DOOR

Story-telling Poems

Selected and Arranged
For Story-telling and Reading Aloud
and for
The Children's Own Reading

BY
FRANCES JENKINS OLCOTT

NEW EDITION, ILLUSTRATED

BOSTON AND NEW YORK
HOUGHTON MIFFLIN COMPANY
The Riverside Press Cambridge
1928

The Riverside Press
CAMBRIDGE · MASSACHUSETTS
PRINTED IN THE U.S.A.

TO

CLARA WHITEHILL HUNT

TO THE STORY-TELLER

There is an inexhaustible source of fine story-telling material to be found in narrative poetry. Fables, myths, legends, tales, romantic or historical in treatment, are told in rhythmic form, and often in a logical manner that makes it easy to retell the plots.

If the story-teller learns her story by reading over and over again a ballad or other story-telling poem, and retells the same in simple prose paraphrase, she will find that her vocabulary is enriched, and that the rhythm of the original lends a swing and added charm to her prose rendering of the poem.

After the story-hour the poem should be read aloud to the children, and they should be encouraged to read it for themselves. In this way the ear may become accustomed to poetic form and expression. Under the direction of a wise teacher, who knows how to correlate her story-telling with reading aloud, the children may be led from the enjoyment of purely narrative poetry to an appreciation of other forms of verse. Thus story-telling poems may be utilized to develop and feed the poetic instinct of children.

In this volume are brought together fables, legends, tales of humor and feeling, of fairy-lore and magic, historical stories, parables, and sacred stories, all told in verse of varying merit.

The rhymes and poems are selected for their story-telling qualities, for their lively interest to children, for their humorous, imaginative, and ethical values, and, as far as possible, for their literary form.

The busy teacher has little time in which to prepare her story, and the young story-teller is confused by detail that leads away from the plot or is unsuitable for children. To meet these needs a few of the poems have been condensed and several others expurgated.

The poems are grouped under subjects, and, as far as possible, are graded so that they may be used with ease in the class rooms of grades one to eight. A full subject index is added so that the story-teller may find, at a glance, lists of poems on different subjects. For example: under the heading *Christmas* may be found a list of poems suitable for use at that season, and under *Courage*, or *Truth-Telling*, are entered poems emphasizing those qualities.

September, 1913.

ACKNOWLEDGMENTS

The compiler's sincere thanks are due the following publishers and authors who have allowed the publication of their poems in this volume: —

To D. Appleton & Co. for permission to use "The Woodman and the Sandal Tree," "The Donkey and the Mocking-Bird," "The White-footed Deer," and "The Elm and the Vine," by William Cullen Bryant; to H. M. Caldwell Company for permission to use "The Rabbi and the Prince," by James Clarence Harvey; to Dana Estes & Co. for permission to use "The Fountain of Youth," by Hezekiah Butterworth; to Little, Brown & Co. for permission to use "King Edwin's Feast," by John W. Chadwick, and "The Parable of St. Christopher" (originally published in *St. Nicholas* Magazine), by Helen Hunt Jackson; to Longmans, Green & Co., for permission to use "The Fairy Boy," from *The Fairy Family;* to The Macmillan Company for permission to use "A Legend of Toledo" and "Harmosan," by Richard Chenevix Trench; to G. P. Putnam's

Sons for permission to use "Rodney's Ride," by E. S. Brooks; to Charles Scribner's Sons for permission to use "Brier-Rose," by H. H. Boyesen, and "The Three Kings of Cologne" and "The White Stag," by Eugene Field; to Houghton Mifflin Company for permission to use many of the poems which are here reprinted; to Miss Edith M. Thomas for permission to use "Babouscka" (originally published in *St. Nicholas* Magazine), from *The Children of Christmas*, published by Richard G. Badger; to Mr. Arthur Guiterman for permission to use "Quivíra."

The compiler wishes also to acknowledge here her indebtedness to Miss Amena Pendleton for valuable suggestions and for her aid in the compilation of this volume.

SEPTEMBER, 1913.

CONTENTS

DEEDS OF RIGHT AND WRONG

FAIRIES, MAGIC, AND MYSTERY

HISTORICAL LEGENDS AND STORIES

The Continent, England, and the United States

Contents

SACRED STORIES AND LEGENDS

ILLUSTRATIONS

Story-telling Poems

Deeds of Right and Wrong

STORY-TELLING POEMS

THE ANT AND THE CRICKET

A SILLY young cricket, accustomed to sing
Through the warm, sunny months of gay
    summer and spring,
Began to complain, when he found that at home
His cupboard was empty and winter was come.
        Not a crumb to be found
        On the snow-covered ground;
        Not a flower could he see,
        Not a leaf on a tree:
"Oh, what will become," says the cricket, "of
    me?"

At last by starvation and famine made bold,
All dripping with wet and all trembling with
    cold,
Away he set off to a miserly ant,
To see if, to keep him alive, he would grant
        Him shelter from rain;
        A mouthful of grain
        He wished only to borrow,
        He'd repay it to-morrow;
If not, he must die of starvation and sorrow.

Says the ant to the cricket: "I'm your servant
  and friend,
But we ants never borrow, we ants never
  lend;
But tell me, dear sir, did you lay nothing by
When the weather was warm?" Said the
  cricket, "Not I.
      My heart was so light
      That I sang day and night,
      For all nature looked gay."
      "You *sang*, sir, you say?
Go then," said the ant, "and *dance* winter
  away."

Thus ending, he hastily lifted the wicket,
And out of the door turned the poor little
  cricket.
Though this is a fable, the moral is good:
If you live without work, you must live with-
  out food.

Anonymous.

THE STORY OF AUGUSTUS WHO WOULD NOT HAVE ANY SOUP

AUGUSTUS was a chubby lad:
Fat ruddy cheeks Augustus had;
And everybody saw with joy,
The plump and hearty, healthy boy.

He ate and drank as he was told,
And never let his soup get cold.
But one day, one cold winter's day,
He scream'd out — "Take the soup away!
O take the nasty soup away!
I won't have any soup to-day!"

How lank and lean Augustus grows!
Next day he scarcely fills his clothes,
Yet, though he feels so weak and ill,
The naughty fellow cries out still —
"Not any soup for me, I say!
O take the nasty soup away!
I won't have any soup to-day!"

The third day comes; oh! what a sin!
To make himself so pale and thin.
Yet, when the soup is put on table,
He screams, as loud as he is able:
"Not any soup for me, I say!
O take the nasty soup away!
I won't have any soup to-day!"

Look at him, now the fourth day's come!
He scarcely weighs a sugar-plum;
He's like a little bit of thread,
And on the fifth day he is — dead!

Dr. Heinrich Hoffmann.

THE SLUGGARD

'T is the voice of the sluggard; I heard him
    complain,
"You have wak'd me too soon, I must slumber
    again;"
As the door on its hinges, so he on his bed,
Turns his sides, and his shoulders, and his
    heavy head.

"A little more sleep and a little more slum-
    ber;"
Thus he wastes half his days, and his hours
    without number;
And when he gets up he sits folding his
    hands,
Or walks about sauntering, or trifling he
    stands.

I passed by his garden, and saw the wild brier,
The thorn and the thistle grow broader and
    higher;
The clothes that hang on him are turning to
    rags;
And his money still wastes, till he starves or
    he begs.

I made him a visit, still hoping to find
That he took better care for improving his
    mind;

He told me his dreams, talked of eating and
  drinking;
But he scarce reads his Bible, and never loves
  thinking.

Said I then to my heart: "Here's a lesson for me;
This man's but a picture of what I might be;
But thanks to my friends for their care in my
  breeding,
Who taught me betimes to love working and
  reading."

Isaac Watts.

FALSE ALARMS

ONE day little Mary most loudly did call:
  "Mamma! O mamma, pray come here,
A fall I have had, oh! a very sad fall!"
  Mamma ran in haste and in fear.
Then Mary jumped up, and she laughed in
  great glee,
  And cried: "Why, how fast you can run!
No harm has befallen, I assure you, to me,
  My screaming was only in fun."

Her mother was busy at work the next day,
  She heard from without a loud cry:
"The great Dog has got me! O help me! O
  pray!
  He tears me, he bites me, I die!"

Mamma, all in terror, quick to the court flew,
  And there little Mary she found;
Who, laughing, said: "Madam, pray how do
    you do?"
  And curtseyed quite down to the ground.

That night little Mary was some time in bed,
  When cries and loud shrieking were heard:
"I'm on fire, O mamma! O come up, or I'm
    dead!"
  Mamma she believed not a word.
"Sleep, sleep, naughty child," she called out
    from below,
  "How often have I been deceived!
You are telling a story, you very well know:
  Go to sleep, for you can't be believed."

Yet still the child screamed; now the house
    filled with smoke.
  "That fire is above," Jane declares.
Alas! Mary's words they soon found were no
    joke,
  When ev'ry one hastened up-stairs.
All burnt and all seamed is her once pretty
    face,
  And terribly marked are her arms,
Her features all scarred, leave a lasting dis-
    grace,
  For giving mamma false alarms.
Adelaide O'Keeffe.

CHARLEY, THE STORY-TELLER

CHARLES was a very wayward youth,
Who to his parents ne'er spoke truth.
"It matters not," thought he, "forsooth,
When no one knows; if I tell lies
They are not written in my eyes!"

His mother once some questions asked,
And artful Charles his cunning tasked;
When loud the parrot chuckling cried:
"You little rogue! may woe betide!
    For, Charley, you've been fibbing!"

Then from the corner comes the cat,
And gives Mamma a gentle pat:
"Good lady, he's deceiving you."
She purrs aloud, "Mew, mew, mew, mew!
    For Charley has been fibbing!"

Down stairs now frightened Charley steals,
As though ten cats were at his heels;
When by his coat Tray seizes him,
And cries: "Bow, wow!" in accents grim,
    "Fie, Charley, you've been fibbing!"

Now both with shame and anger red
That e'en the cock and hens upbraid,
He seeks the garden's safe retreat;

But twittering birds there cry: "Tweat, tweat!
    Fie, Charley, you've been fibbing!"

He runs at last from out the town,
And near a village sits him down;
But even there a fly soon comes,
Who buzzes round his nose and hums:
    "Fie, Charley, you've been fibbing!"

He now the blessed world runs round,
But rest for him is nowhere found;
Go where he will, his ears still greet:
"Mew, mew — bow, wow — buzz, buzz —
    tweat, tweat!
    Fie, Charley, you've been fibbing!"

From the German.

THE TOY OF THE GIANT'S CHILD

BURG NIEDECK is a mountain in Alsace, high
        and strong,
Where once a noble castle stood, — the Giants
        held it long;
Its very ruins now are lost, its site is waste
        and lone,
And if ye seek for Giants there, they all are
        dead and gone.

The Giant's daughter once came forth the
        castle-gate before,

And played, with all a child's delight, beside
    her father's door;
Then sauntering down the precipice, the girl
    did gladly go,
To see, perchance, how matters went, in the
    little world below.

With few and easy steps she passed the moun-
    tain and the wood,
At length near Haslach, at the place where
    mankind dwelt, she stood;
And many a town and village fair, and many a
    field so green,
Before her wondering eyes appeared, a strange
    and curious scene.

And as she gazed, in wonder lost, on all the
    scene around,
She saw a Peasant at her feet, a-tilling of the
    ground;
The little creature crawled about so slowly here
    and there,
And, lighted by the morning sun, his plough
    shone bright and fair.

"Oh, pretty plaything!" cried the child, "I'll
    take thee home with me."
Then with her infant hands she spread her
    kerchief on her knee,

And cradling horse, and man, and plough,
  all gently on her arm,
She bore them home, with cautious steps,
  afraid to do them harm.

She hastes with joyous steps and quick; —
  (we know what children are),
And spying soon her father out, she shouted
  from afar,
"O father, dearest father, such a plaything I
  have found,
I never saw so fair a one on our own mountain
  ground."

Her father sat at table then, and drank his
  wine so mild,
And, smiling with a parent's smile, he asked
  the happy child:
"What struggling creature hast thou brought
  so carefully to me?
Thou leap'st for very joy, my girl; come,
  open, let us see."

She opes her kerchief carefully, and gladly,
  you may deem,
And shows her eager sire the plough, the Peas-
  ant, and his team;
And when she'd placed before his sight the
  new-found pretty toy,

She clasped her hands, and screamed aloud,
　　and cried for very joy.

But her father looked quite seriously, and
　　shaking slow his head:
"What hast thou brought me home, my
　　child? This is no toy," he said,
"Go, take it quickly back again, and put it
　　down below;
The Peasant is no plaything, girl, — how
　　could'st thou think him so?

"Go, go, without a sigh or sob, and do my
　　will," he said,
"For know, without the Peasant, girl, we
　　none of us had bread;
'T is from the Peasant's hardy stock the race
　　of Giants are;
The Peasant is no plaything, child, — no, —
　　God forbid he were!"

From the German of Adelbert von Chamisso.

A STORY FOR A CHILD

LITTLE one, come to my knee!
　　Hark, how the rain is pouring
Over the roof, in the pitch-black night,
　　And the wind in the woods a-roaring!

Hush, my darling, and listen,
　　Then pay for the story with kisses;
Father was lost in the pitch-black night,
　　In just such a storm as this is!

High up on the lonely mountains,
　　Where the wild men watched and waited;
Wolves in the forest, and bears in the bush,
　　And I on my path belated.

The rain and the night together
　　Came down, and the wind came after,
Bending the props of the pine-tree roof,
　　And snapping many a rafter.

I crept along in the darkness,
　　Stunned, and bruised, and blinded, —
Crept to a fir with thick-set boughs,
　　And a sheltering rock behind it.

There, from the blowing and raining,
　　Crouching, I sought to hide me:
Something rustled, two green eyes shone,
　　And a wolf lay down beside me.

Little one, be not frightened;
　　I and the wolf together,
Side by side, through the long, long night
　　Hid from the awful weather.

His wet fur pressed against me;
  Each of us warmed the other;
Each of us felt, in the stormy dark,
  That beast and man was brother.

And when the falling forest
  No longer crashed in warning,
Each of us went from our hiding-place
  Forth in the wild, wet morning.

Darling, kiss me in payment!
  Hark, how the wind is roaring;
Father's house is a better place
  When the stormy rain is pouring!

Bayard Taylor.

THE SPARROWS

In the far-off land of Norway,
  Where the winter lingers late,
And long for the singing-birds and flowers
  The little children wait;

When at last the summer ripens
  And the harvest is gathered in,
And food for the bleak, drear days to come
  The toiling people win;

Through all the land the children
  In the golden fields remain

Till their busy little hands have gleaned
  A generous sheaf of grain;

All the stalks by the reapers forgotten
  They glean to the very least,
To save till the cold December,
  For the sparrows' Christmas feast.

And then through the frost-locked country
  There happens a wonderful thing:
The sparrows flock north, south, east, west,
  For the children's offering.

Of a sudden, the day before Christmas,
  The twittering crowds arrive,
And the bitter, wintry air at once
  With their chirping is all alive.

They perch upon roof and gable,
  On porch and fence and tree,
They flutter about the windows
  And peer in curiously.

And meet the eyes of the children,
  Who eagerly look out
With cheeks that bloom like roses red,
  And greet them with welcoming shout.

On the joyous Christmas morning,
  In front of every door

A tall pole, crowned with clustering grain,
   Is set the birds before.

And which are the happiest, truly
   It would be hard to tell;
The sparrows who share in the Christmas
     cheer,
   Or the children who love them well!

How sweet that they should remember,
   With faith so full and sure,
That the children's bounty awaited them
   The whole wide country o'er!

When this pretty story was told me
   By one who had helped to rear
The rustling grain for the merry birds
   In Norway, many a year,

I thought that our little children
   Would like to know it too,
It seems to me so beautiful,
   So blessed a thing to do,

To make God's innocent creatures see
   In every child a friend,
And on our faithful kindness
   So fearlessly depend.

Celia Thaxter.

GREEDINESS PUNISHED

IT was the cloister Grabow, in the land of
  Usedom,
For years had God's free goodness to fill its
  larder come:
    They might have been contented!

Along the shore came swimming, to give the
  folks good cheer,
Who dwelt within the cloister, two fishes
  every year:
    They might have been contented!

Two sturgeons — two great fat ones; — and
  then this law was set,
That one of them should yearly be taken in a
  net:
    They might have been contented!

The other swam away, then, until next year
  came round,
When, with a new companion, he punctually
  was found:
    They might have been contented!

So then again, they caught one, and served
  him in the dish,

And regularly caught they, year in, year out,
    a fish:
    They might have been contented!

The year, the time appointed *two* such noble
    fishes brought,
The question was a hard one, which of them
    should be caught:
    They might have been contented!

They caught them both together — but every
    greedy wight
Grew sick from over-eating — it served the
    gluttons right; —
    They might have been contented!

This was the least of sorrows — hear how the
    cup ran o'er!
Henceforward, to the cloister no fish came
    swimming more:
    They might have been contented!

So long had God supplied them of his free
    grace alone,
That, now it is denied them, the fault is all
    their own:
    They might have been contented!

    From the German of Friedrich Rückert.

GOD'S JUDGMENT ON A WICKED BISHOP

THE summer and autumn had been so wet
That in winter the corn was growing yet:
'T was a piteous sight to see, all around,
The grain lie rotting on the ground.

Every day the starving poor
Crowded around Bishop Hatto's door;
For he had a plentiful last year's store,
And all the neighborhood could tell
His granaries were furnished well.

At last Bishop Hatto appointed a day
To quiet the poor without delay:
He bade them to his great barn repair,
And they should have food for the winter
    there.

Rejoiced such tidings good to hear,
The poor folk flocked from far and near;
The great barn was full as it could hold
Of women and children, and young and old.

Then, when he saw it could hold no more,
Bishop Hatto he made fast the door;
And while for mercy on Christ they call,
He set fire to the barn, and burnt them all.

"I' faith 't is an excellent bonfire!" quoth he,
"And the country is greatly obliged to me
For ridding it, in these times forlorn,
Of rats that only consume the corn."

So then to his palace returnèd he,
And he sat down to supper merrily,
And he slept that night like an innocent **man**;
But Bishop Hatto never slept again.

In the morning, as he entered the hall
Where his picture hung against the wall,
A sweat like death all over him came,
For the rats had eaten it out of the frame.

As he looked, there came a man from his farm;
He had a countenance white with alarm:
"My lord, I opened your granaries this morn,
And the rats had eaten all your corn."

Another came running presently,
And he was pale as pale could be:
"Fly! my lord bishop, fly!" quoth he.
"Ten thousand rats are coming this **way**:
The Lord forgive you for yesterday!"

"I 'll go to my tower on the Rhine," replied he;
" 'T is the safest place in Germany;
The walls are high, and the shores are steep,
And the stream is strong, and the water deep."

Bishop Hatto fearfully hastened away,
And he crossed the Rhine without delay,
And reached his tower, and barred with
  care
All windows, doors, and loop-holes there.

He laid him down and closed his eyes, —
But soon a scream made him arise,
He started, and saw two eyes of flame
On his pillow, from whence the screaming
  came.

He listened and looked; it was only the cat;
But the Bishop he grew more fearful for that,
For she sat screaming, mad with fear
At the army of rats that were drawing near.

For they have swam over the river so deep,
And they have climbed the shores so steep,
And up the tower their way is bent
To do the work for which they were sent.

They are not to be told by the dozen or
  score,
By thousands they come, and by myriads and
  more;
Such numbers had never been heard of before,
Such a judgment had never been witnessed of
  yore.

Down on his knees the Bishop fell,
And faster and faster his beads did tell,
As louder and louder drawing near
The gnawing of their teeth he could hear.

And in at the windows, and in at the door,
And through the walls helter-skelter they
    pour,
And down from the ceiling, and up through
    the floor,
From the right and the left, from behind and
    before,
From within and without, from above and
    below,
And all at once to the Bishop they go.

They have whetted their teeth against the
    stones,
And now they pick the Bishop's bones;
They gnawed the flesh from every limb,
For they were sent to do judgment on him.

Robert Southey.

THE WHITE-FOOTED DEER

IT was a hundred years ago,
  When, by the woodland ways,
The traveller saw the wild-deer drink,
  Or crop the birchen sprays.

Beneath a hill, whose rocky side
 O'erbrowed a grassy mead,
And fenced a cottage from the wind,
 A deer was wont to feed.

She only came when on the cliffs
 The evening moonlight lay,
And no man knew the secret haunts
 In which she walked by day.

White were her feet, her forehead showed
 A spot of silvery white,
That seemed to glimmer like a star
 In autumn's hazy night.

And here, when sang the whippoorwill,
 She cropped the sprouting leaves,
And here her rustling steps were heard
 On still October eves.

But when the broad midsummer moon
 Rose o'er that grassy lawn,
Beside the silver-footed deer
 There grazed a spotted fawn.

The cottage dame forbade her son
 To aim the rifle here;
"It were a sin," she said, "to harm
 Or fright that friendly deer."

"This spot has been my pleasant home
    Ten peaceful years and more;
And ever, when the moonlight shines,
    She feeds before our door.

"The red-men say that here she walked
    A thousand moons ago;
They never raise the war-whoop here,
    And never twang the bow.

"I love to watch her as she feeds,
    And think that all is well
While such a gentle creature haunts
    The place in which we dwell."

The youth obeyed, and sought for game
    In forests far away,
Where, deep in silence and in moss,
    The ancient woodland lay.

But once, in autumn's golden time
    He ranged the wild in vain,
Nor roused the pheasant nor the deer,
    And wandered home again.

The crescent moon and crimson eve
    Shone with a mingling light;
The deer, upon the grassy mead,
    Was feeding full in sight.

He raised the rifle to his eye,
  And from the cliffs around
A sudden echo, shrill and sharp,
  Gave back its deadly sound.

Away, into the neighboring wood,
  The startled creature flew,
And crimson drops at morning lay
  Amid the glimmering dew.

Next evening shone the waxing moon
  As brightly as before;
The deer upon the grassy mead
  Was seen again no more.

But ere that crescent moon was old,
  By night the red-men came,
And burnt the cottage to the ground,
  And slew the youth and dame.

Now woods have overgrown the mead,
  And hid the cliffs from sight;
There shrieks the hovering hawk at noon,
  And prowls the fox at night.

William Cullen Bryant.

THE INCHCAPE ROCK

No stir in the air, no stir in the sea,
The ship was still as she could be;
Her sails from heaven received no motion;
Her keel was steady in the ocean.

Without either sign or sound of their shock,
The waves flow'd over the Inchcape Rock;
So little they rose, so little they fell,
They did not move the Inchcape Bell.

The Abbot of Aberbrothok
Had placed that Bell on the Inchcape Rock;
On a buoy in the storm it floated and swung,
And over the waves its warning rung.

When the Rock was hid by the surge's swell,
The mariners heard the warning Bell;
And then they knew the perilous Rock,
And blest the Abbot of Aberbrothok.

The Sun in heaven was shining gay;
All things were joyful on that day;
The sea-birds scream'd as they wheel'd round.
And there was joyaunce in their sound.

The buoy of the Inchcape Bell was seen
A darker speck on the ocean green;

Sir Ralph the Rover walk'd his deck,
And he fix'd his eye on the darker speck.

He felt the cheering power of spring;
It made him whistle, it made him sing;
His heart was mirthful to excess,
But the Rover's mirth was wickedness.

His eye was on the Inchcape float;
Quoth he: "My men, put out the boat,
And row me to the Inchcape Rock,
And I'll plague the Abbot of Aberbrothok."

The boat is lower'd, the boatmen row,
And to the Inchcape Rock they go;
Sir Ralph bent over from the boat,
And he cut the Bell from the Inchcape
    float.

Down sunk the Bell with a gurgling sound;
The bubbles rose and burst around;
Quoth Sir Ralph: "The next who comes to the
    Rock
Won't bless the Abbot of Aberbrothok."

Sir Ralph the Rover sail'd away;
He scour'd the seas for many a day;
And now, grown rich with plunder'd store,
He steers his course for Scotland's shore.

So thick a haze o'erspreads the sky;
They cannot see the Sun on high;
The wind hath blown a gale all day;
At evening it hath died away.

On the deck the Rover takes his stand;
So dark it is they see no land.
Quoth Sir Ralph: "It will be lighter soon,
For there is the dawn of the rising Moon."

"Canst hear," said one, "the breakers roar?
For methinks we should be near the shore."
"Now where we are I cannot tell,
But I wish I could hear the Inchcape Bell."

They hear no sound; the swell is strong;
Though the wind hath fallen they drift along,
Till the vessel strikes with a shivering shock,
"O Christ! it is the Inchcape Rock!"

Sir Ralph the Rover tore his hair;
He curst himself in his despair;
The waves rush in on every side;
The ship is sinking beneath the tide.

But even in his dying fear
One dreadful sound could the Rover hear —
A sound as if with the Inchcape Bell
The Devil below was ringing his knell.

Robert Southey.

THE GOOD MAN OF ALLOA

DID you never hear of a queer auld man,
  A very strange man was he,
Who dwelt on the bonnie banks of Forth,
  In a town full dear to me?

One day he sat on a lonely brae,
  And sorely he made his moan,
For his youthful days had pass'd away,
  And ronkilt age came on.

"Ochone, ochone!" quod the poor auld man,
  "Where shall I go lay mine head?
For I am weary of this world,
  And I wish that I were dead.

"For, though I have toil'd these seventy years,
  Wasting both blood and bone,
Striving for riches as for life,
  Yet riches I have none.

"Oh, woe is me! for all my toil,
  And all my dear-bought gains,
Yet must I die a cauldrife death,
  In poverty and pains!

"Oh! where are all my riches gone,
  Where, or to what country!

There is gold enough into this world,
    But none of it made for me.

"Yet Providence was sore misled,
    My riches to destroy,
Else many a poor and virtuous heart
    Should have had cause of joy."

Then the poor auld man laid down his head,
    And rairit for very grief,
And streikit out his limbs to die;
    For he knew of no relief.

But bye there came a lovely dame,
    Upon a palfrey gray,
And she listen'd unto the auld man's tale
    And all he had to say.

Of all his griefs, and sore regret,
    For things that him befell,
And because he could not feed the poor,
    Which thing he loved so well.

"It is great pity," quod the dame,
    "That one so very kind,
So full of charity and love,
    And of such virtuous mind,

"Should lie and perish on a brae,
    Of poverty and eild,

Without one single hand to prove
  His solace and his shield."

She took the auld man her behind
  Upon her palfrey gray,
And swifter nor the southland wind
  They scour'd the velvet brae.

And the palfrey's tail behind did sail
  O'er locker and o'er lea;
While the tears stood in the auld man's eyne,
  With swiftness and with glee;

For the comely dame had promised him
  Of riches mighty store,
That his kind heart might have full scope
  For feeding of the poor.

"Keep thou thy seat," said the comely dame,
  "And conscience clear and stenne;
There is plenty of gold in the sea's bottom
  To enrich ten thousand men.

"Ride on with me, and thou shalt see
  What treasures there do lie;
For I can gallop the emerald wave,
  And along its channels, dry."

And away and away flew the comely dame
  O'er moorland and o'er fell;

But whether they went north or south,
    The auld man could not tell.

And the palfrey's tail behind did sail,
    A comely sight to see,
Like little wee comet of the dale
    Gaun skimmering o'er the lea.

When the auld man came to the salt sea's
        brink,
    He quaked at the ocean faem;
But the palfrey splash'd into the same,
    As it were its native hame.

And the little wee palfrey shot away,
    Like dragon's fiery train,
And up the wave, and down the wave,
    Like meteor of the main.

And its streaming tail behind did sail
    With shimmer and with sheen;
And whenever it struck the mane of the
        wave,
    The flashes of fire were seen.

"Hurrah! hurrah! my bonnie gray!"
    Cried the Maiden of the Sea;
"Ha! thou canst sweep the emerant deep
    Swifter nor bird can flee!

"For thou wast bred in a coral bed,
   Beneath a silver sun,
Where the broad daylight, or the moon by
      night,
   Could never, never won!

"Away! away! my bonnie gray!
   Where billows rock the dead,
And where the richest prize lies low,
   In all the ocean's bed."

And as ever you saw a moudiwort
   Bore into a foggy lea,
So did this little devilish beast
   Dive down into the sea.

The good auld man he gave a rair
   As loud as he could strain:
But the waters closed aboon his head,
   And down he went amain!

But he neither blutherit with his breath,
   Nor gaspit with his ganne,
And not one drop of salt water
   Adown his thropple ran.

At length they came to a gallant ship,
   In the channels of the sea,
That leant her shoulder to a rock,
   With her masts full sore aglee.

It was plain as plain could be,
  From all they saw around,
That the ship had gone down to the deep,
  Without one warning sound.

And there lay many a gallant man,
  Rock'd by the moving main;
And soundly, soundly did they sleep,
  Never to wake again.

So calmly they lay on their glitty beds,
  And in their hammocks swung,
And the billows rock'd their drowsy forms,
  And over their cradles sung.

And there was laid a royal maid,
  As calm as if in heaven,
Who had three gold rings on each finger,
  On her mid finger seven.

And she had jewels in her ears,
  And bracelets brave to see;
The gold that was around her head
  Would have bought earldoms three.

Then the good auld man pull'd out his knife—
  It was both sharp and clear, —
And he cut off the maiden's fingers small,
  And the jewels from ilka ear.

"Oh, shame! oh, shame!" said the Comely
    Dame,
  "Woe worth thy ruthless hand!
How darest thou mangle a royal corpse,
  Once flower of many a land?

"And all for the sake of trinkets vain,
  'Mid such a store as this!"
"Ochone, alake!" quod the good auld man,
  "You judge full far amiss;

"It is better they feed the righteous poor,
  That on their God depend,
Than to lie slumbering in the deep
  For neither use nor end!"

Then the Sea Maid smiled a doubtful smile,
  And said, with lifted ee, —
"Full many a righteous man I have seen,
  But never a one like thee!"

"But thou shalt have thine heart's desire,
  In feeding the upright;
And all the good shall bless the day,
  That first thou saw the light."

Then she loaded him with gems and gold,
  On channel of the main;
Yet the good auld man was not content,
  But turn'd him back again.

And every handful he put in,
    He said right wistfullye,
"Och, this will ane whole fortune prove
    For one poor familye."

And he neifuit in, and he neifuit in,
    And never could refrain,
Quhill the little wee horse he could not move,
    Nor mount the wave again.

"Come away, come away, my little bonnie
        gray,
    Think of the good before;
There is as much gold upon thy back
    As will feed ten thousand poor!"

Then the little wee horse he strauchlit on,
    Through darkling scenes sublime —
O'er shoals, and stones, and dead men's
        bones,
    But the wave he could not climb;

But along, along, he sped along
    The floors of the silent sea,
With a world of waters o'er his head,
    And groves of the coral tree.

And the tide stream flow'd, and the billows
        row'd
    An hundred fathoms high;

And the light that lighted the floors below
  Seem'd from some other sky.

But at length the May, and her palfrey gray,
  And the good auld man beside,
Set their three heads aboon the wave,
  And came in with the flowing tide.

When the little wee horse he found his feet
  On the firm ground and the dry,
He shook his mane, and gave a graen,
  And threw his heels on high.

"Now fare thee well, thou good auld man,
  Thy promise keep in mind;
Let this great wealth I have given to thee
  Be a blessing to thy kind.

"So as thou strive so shalt thou thrive,
  And be it understood
That I must visit thee again,
  For evil or for good."

Then the bonnie May she rode her way
  Along the sea-wave green,
And away and away on her palfrey gray,
  Like the ocean's comely queen.

But it grieveth my heart to tell to you,
  What I never have told before,

Of that man so righteous and so good,
  So long as he was poor;

But, whenever he got more store of gold
  Then ever his wits could tell,
He never would give a mite for good,
  Neither for heaven nor hell.

But he brooded o'er that mighty store
  With sordid heart of sin,
And the houseless wight, or the poor by night,
  His gate wan never within.

And the last accounts I had of him
  Are very strange to tell, —
He was seen with the May and the palfrey
      gray
  Riding fiercely out through hell.

And aye she cried: "Hurrah, hurrah!
  Make room for me and mine!
I bring you the Man of Alloa
  To his punishment condign!

"His Maker tried him in the fire,
  To make his heart contrite;
But, when he gat his heart's desire,
  He proved a hypocrite!"
                    (*Condensed.*) *James Hogg.*

THE ELM AND THE VINE

"Uphold my feeble branches
  By thy strong arms, I pray."
Thus to the Elm her neighbor
  The Vine was heard to say.

"Else, lying low and helpless,
  A wretched lot is mine,
Crawled o'er by every reptile,
  And browsed by hungry kine."

The Elm was moved to pity.
  Then spoke the generous tree:
"My hapless friend, come hither,
  And find support in me."

The kindly Elm, receiving
  The grateful Vine's embrace,
Became, with that adornment,
  The garden's pride and grace;

Became the chosen covert
  In which the wild birds sing;
Became the love of shepherds,
  And glory of the spring.

(Condensed.) From the Spanish of José Rosas.
Translated by William Cullen Bryant.

THE GOURD AND THE PALM
(*A Persian Fable*)

"How old art thou?" said the garrulous
    gourd,
As o'er the palm-tree's crest it poured
Its spreading leaves and tendrils fine,
And hung a bloom in the morning shine.
"A hundred years!" the palm-tree sighed:
"And *I*," the saucy gourd replied,
"Am at the most a hundred hours,
And overtop thee in the bowers!"

Through all the palm-tree's leaves there went
A tremor as of self-content.
"I live my life," it whispering said,
"See what I see, and count the dead;
And every year, of all I've known,
A gourd above my head has grown,
And made a boast, like thine to-day;
Yet here *I* stand — but where are *they*?"

Anonymous.

THE PLUCKY PRINCE

There was a youthful scion
Of a race of tyrant kings,
Who roused his father's anger
By the way he wasted things.

Quoth then the wrathful monarch:
"Quick from my presence flee!
Yet turn your heedless ear
To this my stern decree:
No fish or flesh or fowl
Shall your hunger's needs supply.
Nor beast nor worm contribute
To the clothing which you buy.
When comes the gloomy night-time,
No oil or vapor light,
No wax or tallow candle,
Shall make the darkness bright.
Nor grains upon the hill-side,
Nor tuberous roots on earth,
Nor fruitful vines, and juicy,
Contribute to your mirth.
    Thou prodigal! Avaunt!
Go, starve upon the plain!
Thou never, nevermore,
Shalt waste my wealth again."

    His son this law of exile
Conned over at his ease:
"He has," he said, "left to me
The mighty help of *trees*."
He gayly snapped his fingers,
He slammed the palace door —
"Stern monarch, I shall flourish
As proudly as before!"

A house he quickly builded:
It all was wondrous fine;
Of English oak its rafters,
Its floors of Norway pine.
On pillars of palmetto
The cypress-shingled roof,
With oaken eaves and gargoyles,
Against the storms was proof.
There curious palm-mattings
Spread over all the floors,
Dyed crimson with the logwood
From warm Caribbean shores.
Quaint furniture of walnut
And perfumed sandal-wood,
With highly polished rose-wood,
Throughout the mansion stood.
"Now," said this Prince complaisant,
"A ball I mean to give,
I'll show the King, my father,
How finely I can live!"

The night came on apace
When the house was light as day,
For candle-nuts in sconces
Shed many a golden ray.
Magnolias from the South land,
Pink apple-blooms from Maine,
All vied with orange-flowers
The subtlest sense to chain.

The noted guests assembled
Found waiting for them all
A fairer feast than ever
Graced kingly banquet-hall.
For dishes, carved in queer ways
That haunt the Chinese mind,
Bore nuts and fruits from every land
Familiar to mankind.

Cassava cakes from Java,
The solid plantain's meat,
With chocolate were proffered,
And maple-sugar sweet.
Fair pomegranates and soursops,
With luscious guava jam,
Stood near the odious durion
From islands near Siam.
Bananas, figs, and lemons,
Dates, cherries, plums and pears,
All seemed so *very common*
One passed them unawares.

Amid this festive splendor
The Prince received his guest;
In robes of cocoa woven
He was superbly drest,
While from the crown of laurels
His realm placed on his brow,

Down to his shoes of caoutchouc,
He looked a king, I trow.
"Warm welcomes to my mansion!" —
'T was thus he met the King —
"See what a man you made me
By your cold banishing!"

A genial smile illumined
The monarch and his train.
"O Prince! of you I'm very proud —
Come to my arms again!"
So spake the King, embracing
His enterprising son,
And then, with jokes and laughter
The banquet was begun.
The court drank so much cider
They complimentary grew;
While the King declared the cashew
Was the finest wine he knew.
To this the Premier added,
He hoped the Prince would grow
Like to the giant banyan,
And live long here below.
Then soon the party ended,
The guests all said: "Farewell,"
And the wonders of the woodland
They hastened home to tell.

May Bryant.

APPLE-SEED JOHN

POOR Johnny was bended well nigh double
With years of toil, and care, and trouble;
But his large old heart still felt the need
Of doing for others some kindly deed.

"But what can I do?" old Johnny said:
"I who work so hard for daily bread?
It takes heaps of money to do much good;
I am far too poor to do as I would."

The old man sat thinking deeply a while,
Then over his features gleamed a smile,
And he clapped his hands with a boyish glee,
And said to himself: "There's a way for me!"

He worked, and he worked with might and
      main,
But no one knew the plan in his brain.
He took ripe apples in pay for chores,
And carefully cut from them all the cores.

He filled a bag full, then wandered away,
And no man saw him for many a day.
With knapsack over his shoulder slung,
He marched along, and whistled or sung.

He seemed to roam with no object in view,
Like one who had nothing on earth to do;

But, journeying thus o'er the prairies wide,
He paused now and then, and his bag untied.

With pointed cane deep holes he would bore,
And in every hole he placed a core;
Then covered them well, and left them there
In keeping of sunshine, rain, and air.

Sometimes for days he waded through grass,
And saw not a living creature pass,
But often, when sinking to sleep in the dark,
He heard the owls hoot and the prairie-dogs
    bark.

Sometimes an Indian of sturdy limb
Came striding along and walked with him;
And he who had food shared with the other,
As if he had met a hungry brother.

When the Indian saw how the bag was filled,
And looked at the holes that the white man
    drilled,
He thought to himself 't was a silly plan
To be planting seed for some future man.

Sometimes a log cabin came in view,
Where Johnny was sure to find jobs to do,
By which he gained stores of bread and meat,
And welcome rest for his weary feet.

He had full many a story to tell,
And goodly hymns that he sung right well;
He tossed up the babes, and joined the boys
In many a game full of fun and noise.

And he seemed so hearty, in work or play,
Men, women, and boys all urged him to stay;
But he always said: "I have something to do,
And I must go on to carry it through."

The boys, who were sure to follow him round,
Soon found what it was he put in the ground;
And so, as time passed and he traveled on,
Ev'ry one called him "Old Apple-Seed John."

Whenever he'd used the whole of his store,
He went into cities and worked for more;
Then he marched back to the wilds again,
And planted seed on hill-side and plain.

In cities, some said the old man was crazy;
While others said he was only lazy;
But he took no notice of gibes and jeers,
He knew he was working for future years.

He knew that trees would soon abound
Where once a tree could not have been found;
That a flick'ring play of light and shade
Would dance and glimmer along the glade;

That blossoming sprays would form fair bowers,
And sprinkle the grass with rosy showers;
And the little seeds his hands had spread,
Would become ripe apples when he was dead.

So he kept on traveling far and wide,
Till his old limbs failed him, and he died.
He said at the last: " 'T is a comfort to feel
I've done good in the world, though not a
        great deal."

Weary travelers, journeying west,
In the shade of his trees find pleasant rest;
And they often start, with glad surprise,
At the rosy fruit that round them lies.

And if they inquire whence came such trees,
Where not a bough once swayed in the breeze,
The answer still comes, as they travel on:
"These trees were planted by Apple-Seed
        John."

Lydia Maria Child.

THE WOODMAN AND THE
SANDAL TREE

Beside a sandal tree a woodman stood
    And swung the axe, and while its blows were
        laid
Upon the fragrant trunk, the generous wood

With its own sweet perfumed the cruel blade.
Go, then, and do the like. A soul endued
  With light from Heaven, a nature pure and
     great,
Will place its highest bliss in doing good,
And good for evil give, and love for hate.

From the Spanish of José Rosas,
Translated by William Cullen Bryant.

THE BELL OF ATRI

At Atri in Abruzzo, a small town
Of ancient Roman date, but scant renown,
One of those little places that have run
Half up the hill, beneath a blazing sun,
And then sat down to rest, as if to say,
"I climb no farther upward, come what
     may," —
The Re Giovanni, now unknown to fame,
So many monarchs since have borne the name,
Had a great bell hung in the market-place,
Beneath a roof, projecting some small space
By way of shelter from the sun and rain.
Then rode he through the streets with all his
     train,
And, with the blast of trumpets loud and long,
Made proclamation, that whenever wrong
Was done to any man, he should but ring
The great bell in the square, and he, the King,

Would cause the Syndic to decide thereon.
Such was the proclamation of King John.

How swift the happy days in Atri sped,
What wrongs were righted, need not here be
        said.
Suffice it that, as all things must decay,
The hempen rope at length was worn away,
Unravelled at the end, and, strand by strand,
Loosened and wasted in the ringer's hand,
Till one, who noted this in passing by,
Mended the rope with braids of briony,
So that the leaves and tendrils of the vine
Hung like a votive garland at a shrine.

By chance it happened that in Atri dwelt
A knight, with spur on heel and sword in belt,
Who loved to hunt the wild-boar in the woods,
Who loved his falcons with their crimson
        hoods,
Who loved his hounds and horses, and all
        sports
And prodigalities of camps and courts; —
Loved, or had loved them; for at last, grown
        old,
His only passion was the love of gold.

He sold his horses, sold his hawks and hounds,
Rented his vineyards and his garden-grounds,

Kept but one steed, his favorite steed of all,
To starve and shiver in a naked stall,
And day by day sat brooding in his chair,
Devising plans how best to hoard and spare.

At length he said: "What is the use or need
To keep at my own cost this lazy steed,
Eating his head off in my stables here,
When rents are low and provender is dear?
Let him go feed upon the public ways;
I want him only for the holidays."
So the old steed was turned into the heat
Of the long, lonely, silent, shadeless street;
And wandered in suburban lanes forlorn,
Barked at by dogs, and torn by brier and
        thorn.

One afternoon, as in that sultry clime
It is the custom in the summer time,
With bolted doors and window-shutters
        closed,
The inhabitants of Atri slept or dozed;
When suddenly upon their senses fell
The loud alarm of the accusing bell!
The Syndic started from his deep repose,
Turned on his couch, and listened, and then
        rose
And donned his robes, and with reluctant pace
Went panting forth into the market-place,

Where the great bell upon its cross-beams
    swung,
Reiterating with persistent tongue,
In half-articulate jargon, the old song:
"Some one hath done a wrong, hath done a
    wrong!"

But ere he reached the belfry's light arcade
He saw, or thought he saw, beneath its shade,
No shape of human form of woman born,
But a poor steed dejected and forlorn,
Who with uplifted head and eager eye
Was tugging at the vines of briony.
"Domeneddio!" cried the Syndic straight,
"This is the Knight of Atri's steed of state!
He calls for justice, being sore distressed,
And pleads his cause as loudly as the best."

Meanwhile from street and lane a noisy crowd
Had rolled together like a summer cloud,
And told the story of the wretched beast
In five-and-twenty different ways at least,
With much gesticulation and appeal
To heathen gods, in their excessive zeal.
The Knight was called and questioned; in
    reply
Did not confess the fact, did not deny;
Treated the matter as a pleasant jest,
And set at naught the Syndic and the rest,

Maintaining, in an angry undertone,
That he should do what pleased him with his
    own.

And thereupon the Syndic gravely read
The proclamation of the King; then said:
"Pride goeth forth on horseback grand and
    gay,
But cometh back on foot, and begs its way;
Fame is the fragrance of heroic deeds,
Of flowers of chivalry and not of weeds!
These are familiar proverbs; but I fear
They never yet have reached your knightly
    ear.
What fair renown, what honor, what repute
Can come to you from starving this poor
    brute?
He who serves well and speaks not, merits
    more
Than they who clamor loudest at the door.
Therefore the law decrees that as this steed
Served you in youth, henceforth you shall
    take heed
To comfort his old age, and to provide
Shelter in stall, and food and field beside."
The Knight withdrew abashed; the people all
Led home the steed in triumph to his stall.
The King heard and approved, and laughed
    in glee,

And cried aloud: "Right well it pleaseth me!
Church-bells at best but ring us to the doors;
But go not into mass; my bell doth more:
It cometh into court and pleads the cause
Of creatures dumb and unknown to the laws;
And this shall make, in every Christian clime,
The Bell of Atri famous for all time."

Henry Wadsworth Longfellow.

TUBAL CAIN

I

OLD TUBAL CAIN was a man of might
  In the days when the earth was young;
By the fierce red light of his furnace bright,
  The strokes of his hammer rung;
And he lifted high his brawny hand
  On the iron glowing clear,
Till the sparks rushed out in scarlet showers,
  As he fashioned the sword and the spear.
And he sang: "Hurrah for my handiwork!
  Hurrah for the Spear and Sword!
Hurrah for the hand that shall wield them well,
  For he shall be king and lord!"

II

To Tubal Cain came many a one,
  As he wrought by his roaring fire,

And each one prayed for a strong steel blade
  As the crown of his desire;
And he made them weapons sharp and strong,
  Till they shouted loud for glee,
And gave him gifts of pearl and gold,
  And spoils of the forest free.
And they sang: "Hurrah for Tubal Cain,
  Who hath given us strength anew!
Hurrah for the smith, hurrah for the fire,
  And hurrah for the metal true!"

III

But a sudden change came o'er his heart,
  Ere the setting of the sun,
And Tubal Cain was filled with pain
  For the evil he had done;
He saw that men, with rage and hate,
  Made war upon their kind;
That the land was red with the blood they
      shed
  In their lust for carnage blind.
And he said: "Alas! that ever I made,
  Or that skill of mine should plan,
The spear and the sword for men whose joy
  Is to slay their fellow-man!"

IV

And for many a day old Tubal Cain
  Sat brooding o'er his woe;

And his hand forbore to smite the ore,
  And his furnace smouldered low.
But he rose at last with a cheerful face,
  And a bright courageous eye,
And bared his strong right arm for work,
  While the quick flames mounted high.
And he sang: "Hurrah for my handiwork!"
  And the red sparks lit the air;
"Not alone for the blade was the bright steel
      made;" —
  As he fashioned the First Ploughshare!

v

And men, taught wisdom from the Past,
  In friendship joined their hands,
Hung the sword in the hall, the spear on the
      wall,
  And ploughed the willing lands,
And sang: "Hurrah for Tubal Cain!
  Our staunch good friend is he;
And for the ploughshare and the plough
  To him our praise shall be.
But while Oppression lifts its head,
  Or a tyrant would be lord,
Though we may thank him for the Plough,
  We'll not forget the Sword!"
Charles Mackay.

BRIER–ROSE

Part I

SAID Brier-Rose's mother to the naughty
    Brier-Rose:
"What *will* become of you, my child, the Lord
    Almighty knows.
You will not scrub the kettles, and you will
    not touch the broom;
You never sit a minute still at spinning-wheel
    or loom."

Thus grumbled in the morning, and grumbled
    late at eve,
The good-wife as she bustled with pot and
    tray and sieve;
But Brier-Rose, she laughed and she cocked
    her dainty head:
"Why, I shall marry, Mother dear," full
    merrily she said.

"*You* marry, saucy Brier-Rose! The man, he
    is not found
To marry such a worthless wench, these seven
    leagues around."
But Brier-Rose, she laughed and she trilled a
    merry lay:
"Perhaps he'll come, my Mother dear, from
    eight leagues away."

Up stole the girl on tiptoe, so that none her
    step could hear,
And laughing pressed an airy kiss behind the
    good-wife's ear.
And she, as e'er relenting, sighed: "Oh,
    Heaven only knows
Whatever will become of you, my naughty
    Brier-Rose!"

.   .   .   .

The sun was high and summer sounds were
    teeming in the air;
The clank of scythes, the cricket's whir, and
    swelling wood-notes rare,
From field and copse and meadow; and
    through the open door
Sweet, fragrant whiffs of new-mown hay the
    idle breezes bore.

And out she skipped the meadows o'er and
    gazed into the sky;
Her heart o'er brimmed with gladness, she
    scarce herself knew why,
And to a merry tune she hummed: "Oh,
    Heaven only knows
Whatever will become of the naughty Brier-
    Rose!"

Whene'er a thrifty matron this idle maid
    espied,

She shook her head in warning, and scarce her
    wrath could hide;
For girls were made for housewives, for spin-
    ning-wheel and loom,
And not to drink the sunshine and wild-
    flower's sweet perfume.

And oft the maidens cried, when the Brier-
    Rose went by;
"You cannot knit a stocking, and you cannot
    make a pie."
But Brier-Rose, as was her wont, she cocked
    her curly head:
"But I can sing a pretty song," full merrily
    she said.

And oft the young lads shouted, when they
    saw the maid at play:
"Ho, good-for-nothing Brier-Rose, how do
    you do to-day?"
Then she shook her tiny fist; to her cheeks
    the color flew:
"However much you coax me, I'll *never* dance
    with you!"

Part II

Thus flew the years light-wingèd over Brier-
    Rose's head,
Till she was twenty summers old, and yet
    remained unwed.

And all the parish wondered: "The Lord
    Almighty knows
Whatever will become of that naughty Brier-
    Rose!"

And while they wondered came the Spring
    a-dancing o'er the hills;
Her breath was warmer than of yore, and all
    the mountain rills,
With their tinkling and their rippling and
    their rushing, filled the air,
And the misty sounds of water forth-welling
    everywhere.

And in the valley's depth, like a lusty beast
    of prey,
The river leaped and roared aloud and tossed
    its mane of spray;
Then hushed again its voice to a softly plash-
    ing croon,
As dark it rolled beneath the sun and white
    beneath the moon.

It was a merry sight to see the lumber as it
    whirled
Adown the tawny eddies that hissed and
    seethed and swirled,
Now shooting through the rapids and, with a
    reeling swing,
Into the foam-crests diving like an animated
    thing.

But in the narrows of the rocks, where o'er a
    steep incline
The waters plunged, and wreathed in foam
    the dark boughs of the pine,
The lads kept watch with shout and song, and
    sent each straggling beam
A-spinning down the rapids, lest it should
    lock the stream.

Part III

And yet — methinks I hear it now, — wild
    voices in the night,
A rush of feet, a dog's harsh bark, a torch's
    flaring light,
And wandering gusts of dampness, and 'round
    us far and nigh,
A throbbing boom of water like a pulse-beat
    in the sky.

The dawn just pierced the pallid east with
    spears of gold and red,
As we, with boat-hooks in our hands, toward
    the narrows sped.
And terror smote us; for we heard the mighty
    tree-tops sway,
And thunder, as of chariots, and hissing
    showers of spray.

"Now, lads," the sheriff shouted, "you are
    strong, like Norway's rock:
A hundred crowns I give to him who breaks
    the lumber-lock!
For if another hour go by, the angry waters'
    spoil
Our homes will be, and fields, and our weary
    years of toil!"

We looked each at the other; each hoped his
    neighbor would
Brave death and danger for his home, as
    valiant Norsemen should.
But at our feet the brawling tide expanded
    like a lake,
And whirling beams came shooting on, and
    made the firm rock quake.

"Two hundred crowns," the sheriff cried,
    and breathless stood the crowd.
"Two hundred crowns, my bonny lads!" in
    anxious tones and loud.
But not a man came forward, and no one
    spoke or stirred,
And nothing save the thunder of the cataract
    was heard.

But as with trembling hands, and with faint-
    ing hearts we stood,

We spied a little curly head emerging from
    the wood.
We heard a little snatch of a merry little
    song,
And saw the dainty Brier-Rose come dancing
    through the throng.

An angry murmur rose from the people round
    about:
"Fling her into the river," we heard the
    matrons shout,
"Chase her away, the silly thing; for God
    Himself scarce knows
Why ever He created that worthless Brier-
    Rose!"

Sweet Brier-Rose, she heard their cries; a
    little pensive smile
Across her fair face flitted that might a stone
    beguile;
And then she gave her pretty head a roguish
    little cock:
"Hand me a boat-hook, lads," she said, "I
    think I'll break the lock."

Derisive shouts of laughter broke from throats
    of young and old:
"Ho! good-for-nothing Brier-Rose, your
    tongue was ever bold."

And, mockingly, a boat-hook into her hands
          was flung,
When, lo! into the river's midst with daring
          leaps she sprung!

We saw her dimly through a mist of dense
          and blinding spray;
From beam to beam she skipped, like a water-
          sprite at play.
And now and then faint gleams we caught of
          color through the mist;
A crimson waist, a golden head, a little dainty
          wrist.

In terror pressed the people to the margin
          of the hill,
A hundred breaths were bated, a hundred
          hearts stood still.
For, hark! from out the rapids came a strange
          and creaking sound,
And then a crash of thunder which shook the
          very ground.

The waters hurled the lumber mass down o'er
          the rocky steep.
We heard a muffled rumbling and a rolling
          in the deep;
We saw a tiny form which the torrent swiftly
          bore
And flung into the wild abyss, where it was
          seen no more.

Ah, little naughty Brier-Rose, thou couldst
    nor weave nor spin;
Yet thou couldst do a nobler deed than all
    thy mocking kin;
For thou hadst courage e'en to die, and by
    thy death to save
A thousand farms and lives from the fury of
    the wave.

        (Condensed.)   *Hjalmar Hjorth Boyesen.*

THE KNIGHT'S TOAST

THE feast is o'er! Now brimming wine
In lordly cup is seen to shine
  Before each eager guest;
And silence fills the crowded hall,
As deep as when the herald's call
  Thrills in the loyal breast.

Then up arose the noble host,
And smiling cried: "A toast! a toast!
  To all our ladies fair!
Here, before all, I pledge the name
Of Staunton's proud and beauteous dame, —
  The lady Gundamere!"

Then to his feet each gallant sprung,
And joyous was the shout that rung,
  As Stanley gave the word;

And every cup was raised on high,
Nor ceased the loud and gladsome cry,
  Till Stanley's voice was heard.

"Enough, enough," he smiling said,
And lowly bent his haughty head,
  "That all may have their due,
Now each in turn must play his part,
And pledge the lady of his heart,
  Like gallant knight and true!"

Then one by one each guest sprung up,
And drained in turn the brimming cup,
  And named the loved one's name;
And each, as hand on high he raised,
His lady's grace or beauty praised,
  Her constancy and fame.

'T is now St. Leon's turn to rise;
On him are fixed those countless eyes; —
  A gallant knight is he;
Envied by some, admired by all,
Far-famed in lady's bower and hall, —
  The flower of chivalry.

St. Leon raised his kindling eye,
And lifts the sparkling cup on high;
  "I drink to one," he said,

"Whose image never may depart,
Deep graven on this grateful heart,
    Till memory be dead.

"To one whose love for me shall last
When lighter passions long have passed,
    So holy 't is and true;
To one whose love hath longer dwelt,
More deeply fixed, more keenly felt,
    Than any pledged by you!"

Each guest upstarted at the word,
And laid a hand upon his sword,
    With fury-flashing eye;
And Stanley said: "We crave the name,
Proud knight, of this most peerless dame,
    Whose love you count so high."

St. Leon paused, as if he would
Not breathe her name in careless mood,
    Thus, lightly, to another;
Then bent his noble head, as though
To give that word the reverence due,
    And gently said: "*My Mother!*"

Attributed to Sir Walter Scott.

THE GLOVE AND THE LIONS

King Francis was a hearty king, and loved a
    royal sport,
And one day as his lions fought, sat looking on
    the court;
The nobles filled the benches, and the ladies
    in their pride,
And 'mongst them sat the Count de Lorge,
    with one for whom he sighed:
And truly 't was a gallant thing to see that
    crowning show,
Valor and love, and a king above, and the
    royal beasts below.

Ramp'd and roar'd the lions, with horrid
    laughing jaws;
They bit, they glared, gave blows like beams,
    a wind went with their paws;
With wallowing might and stifled roar they
    rolled on one another,
Till all the pit with sand and mane was in a
    thunderous smother;
The bloody foam above the bars came whisk-
    ing through the air;
Said Francis then: "Faith, gentlemen, we're
    better here than there."

De Lorge's love o'erheard the King,—a
    beauteous lively dame
With smiling lips and sharp bright eyes, which
    always seem'd the same:
She thought, "The Count, my lover, is brave
    as brave can be;
He surely would do wondrous things to show
    his love of me;
King, ladies, lovers, all look on; the occasion is
    divine;
I'll drop my glove, to prove his love; great
    glory will be mine."

She dropp'd her glove, to prove his love, then
    look'd at him and smiled;
He bowed, and in a moment leapt among the
    lions wild:
The leap was quick, return was quick, he has
    regain'd his place,
Then threw the glove, but not with love, right
    in the lady's face.
"Well done!" cried Francis, "rightly done!"
    and he rose from where he sat:
"No love," quoth he, "but vanity, sets love
    a task like that."

Leigh Hunt.

OPPORTUNITY

This I beheld, or dreamed it in a dream: —
There spread a cloud of dust along the plain;
And underneath the cloud, or in it, raged
A furious battle, and men yelled, and swords
Shocked upon swords and shields. A prince's
      banner
Wavered, then staggered backward, hemmed
      by foes.
A craven hung along the battle's edge,
And thought: "Had I a sword of keener steel —
That blue blade that the King's son bears, —
      but this
Blunt thing —!" he snapt and flung it from
      his hand,
And lowering crept away and left the field.
Then came the King's son, wounded, sore
      bestead,
And weaponless, and saw the broken sword,
Hilt-buried in the dry and trodden sand,
And ran and snatched it, and with battle-
      shout
Lifted afresh he hewed his enemy down,
And saved a great cause that heroic day.

Edward Rowland Sill.

YUSSOUF

A STRANGER came one night to Yussouf's tent,
Saying: "Behold one outcast and in dread,
Against whose life the bow of power is bent,
Who flies, and hath not where to lay his head;
I come to thee for shelter and for food,
To Yussouf, called through all our tribes
    'The Good.'"

"This tent is mine," said Yussouf, "but no
    more
Than it is God's; come in, and be at peace;
Freely shalt thou partake of all my store
As I of His who buildeth over these
Our tents His glorious roof of night and day,
And at whose door none ever yet heard Nay."

So Yussouf entertained his guest that night,
And, waking him ere day, said: "Here is gold;
My swiftest horse is saddled for thy flight;
Depart before the prying day grow bold."
As one lamp lights another, nor grows less,
So nobleness enkindleth nobleness.

That inward light the stranger's face made
    grand,
Which shines from all self-conquest; kneeling
    low,

He bowed his forehead upon Yussouf's hand,
Sobbing: "O Sheik, I cannot leave thee so;
I will repay thee; all this thou hast done
Unto that Ibrahim who slew thy son!"

"Take thrice the gold," said Yussouf, "for
    with thee
Into the desert, never to return,
My one black thought shall ride away from
    me;
First-born, for whom by day and night I
    yearn,
Balanced and just are all of God's decrees;
Thou art avenged, my first-born, sleep in
    peace!"

James Russell Lowell.

JAFFÁR

JAFFÁR, the Barmecide, the good Vizier,
The poor man's hope, the friend without a
    peer.
Jaffár was dead, slain by a doom unjust;
And guilty Hároun, sullen with mistrust
Of what the good, and e'en the bad might say,
Ordain'd that no man living from that day
Should dare to speak his name on pain of
    death.
All Araby and Persia held their breath.

All but the brave Mondeer. — He, proud to
    show
How far for love a grateful soul could go,
And facing death for very scorn and grief,
(For his great heart wanted a great relief,)
Stood forth in Bagdad, daily, in the square
Where once had stood a happy house; and
    there
Harangued the tremblers at the scimitar
On all they owed to the divine Jaffár.
"Bring me this man," the Caliph cried. The
    man
Was brought, was gazed upon. The mutes
    began
To bind his arms. "Welcome, brave cords,"
    cried he;
"From bonds far worse Jaffár deliver'd me;
From wants, from shames, from loveless house-
    hold fears;
Made a man's eyes friends with delicious
    tears;
Restor'd me, loved me, put me on a par
With his great self. How can I pay Jaffár?"
Hároun, who felt that on a soul like this
The mightiest vengeance could but fall amiss,
Now deigned to smile, as one great lord of
    fate
Might smile upon another half as great.
He said: "Let worth grow frenzied if it will;

The Caliph's judgment shall be master still.
Go; and since gifts thus move thee, take this
    gem,
The richest in the Tartar's diadem,
And hold the giver as thou deemest fit."
"Gifts!" cried the friend. He took; and hold-
    ing it
High towards the heavens, as though to meet
    his star
Exclaimed, "This, too, I owe to thee, Jaffár!"
Leigh Hunt.

HARMOSAN

Now the third and fatal conflict for the Per-
    sian throne was done,
And the Moslem's fiery valor had the crown-
    ing victory won.

Harmosan, the last and boldest the invader to
    defy,
Captive, overborne by numbers, they were
    bringing forth to die.

Then exclaimed that noble captive: "Lo, I
    perish in my thirst!
Give me but one drink of water, and let then
    arrive the worst!"

In his hand he took the goblet; but a while
    the draught forbore,
Seeming doubtfully the purpose of the foemen
    to explore.

Well might then have paused the bravest —
    for around him angry foes
With a hedge of naked weapons did that
    lonely man enclose.

"But what fear'st thou?" cried the Caliph,
    "is it, friend, a secret blow?
Fear it not! our gallant Moslem no such treach-
    erous dealing know.

"Thou may'st quench thy thirst securely, for
    thou shalt not die before
Thou hast drunk that cup of water; this re-
    prieve is thine — no more!"

Quick the Satrap dashed the goblet down to
    earth with ready hand,
And the liquid sank forever, lost amid the
    burning sand.

"Thou hast said that mine my life is, till the
    water of that cup
I have drained: then bid thy servants that
    spilt water gather up!"

For a moment stood the Caliph as by doubt-
    ful passions stirred —
Then exclaimed: "Forever sacred must re-
    main a monarch's word!

"Bring another cup and straightway to the
    noble Persian give;
Drink, I said before, and perish — now I bid
    thee, drink and live!"

Richard Chenevix Trench.

THE TWO CHURCH-BUILDERS

A famous King would build a church,
    A temple vast and grand;
And, that the praise might be his own,
    He gave a strict command
That none should add the smallest gift
    To aid the work he planned.

And when the mighty dome was done,
    Within the noble frame,
Upon a tablet broad and fair,
    In letters all aflame
With burnished gold, the people read
    The royal builder's name.

Now, when the King, elate with pride,
    That night had sought his bed,

He dreamed he saw an Angel come
  (A halo round his head,)
Erase the royal name, and write
  Another in its stead.

What could it mean? Three times that
    night
  That wondrous vision came;
Three times he saw that Angel hand
  Erase the royal name,
And write a woman's in its stead,
  In letters all aflame.

Whose could it be? He gave command
  To all about his throne,
To seek the owner of the name
  That on the tablet shone;
And so it was the courtiers found
  A widow poor and lone.

The King, enraged at what he heard,
  Cried: "Bring the culprit here!"
And to the woman, trembling sore,
  He said: "'T is very clear
That you have broken my command;
  Now let the truth appear!"

"Your majesty," the widow said:
  "I can't deny the truth;

I love the Lord, — my Lord and yours, —
And so, in simple sooth,
I broke your majesty's command
(I crave your royal ruth).

"And since I had no money, sire,
Why, I could only pray
That God would bless your majesty;
And when along the way
The horses drew the stones, I gave
To one a wisp of hay."

"Ah! now I see," the King exclaimed,
"Self-glory was my aim;
The woman gave for love of God,
And not for worldly fame!
'T is my command the tablet bear
The pious widow's name."

John G. Saxe.

SIR LAUNFAL AND THE LEPER

As Sir Launfal made morn through the dark-
some gate,
He was 'ware of a leper, crouched by the
same,
Who begged with his hand and moaned as he
sate;
And a loathing over Sir Launfal came;

The sunshine went out of his soul with a thrill,
  The flesh 'neath his armor 'gan shrink and
    crawl,
And midway its leap his heart stood still
  Like a frozen waterfall;
For this man, so foul and bent of stature,
Rasped harshly against his dainty nature,
And seemed the one blot on the summer
    morn, —
So he tossed him a piece of gold in scorn.

The leper raised not the gold from the dust:
"Better to me the poor man's crust,
Better the blessing of the poor,
Though I turn me empty from his door;
That is no true alms which the hand can hold:
He gives only the worthless gold
  Who gives from a sense of duty;
But he who gives but a slender mite,
And gives to that which is out of sight,
  That thread of the all-sustaining Beauty
Which runs through all and doth all unite, —
The hand cannot clasp the whole of his alms,
The heart outstretches its eager palms,
For a god goes with it and makes it store
To the soul that was starving in darkness
    before."

James Russell Lowell.

FAIRIES, MAGIC, AND MYSTERY

THE DORCHESTER GIANT

THERE was a Giant in time of old,
A mighty one was he;
He had a wife, but she was a scold,
So he kept her shut in his mammoth fold;
And he had children three.

It happened to be an election day,
And the giants were choosing a king;
The people were not democrats then,
They did not talk of the rights of men,
And all that sort of thing.

Then the Giant took his children three,
And fastened them in the pen;
The children roared; quoth the Giant: "Be
    still!"
And Dorchester Heights and Milton Hill
Rolled back the sound again.

Then he brought them a pudding stuffed with
    plums,
As big as the State-House dome;
Quoth he: "There's something for you to eat;
So stop your mouths with your 'lection treat,
And wait till your dad comes home."

So the Giant pulled him a chestnut stout,
And whittled the boughs away;
The boys and their mother set up a shout;
Said he, "You're in, and you can't get out,
Bellow as loud as you may."

Off he went, and he growled a tune
As he strode the fields along;
'T is said a buffalo fainted away,
And fell as cold as a lump of clay,
When he heard the Giant's song. —

What are those lone ones doing now,
The wife and the children sad?
Oh, they are in a terrible rout,
Screaming, and throwing their pudding about,
Acting as they were mad.

They flung it over to Roxbury hills,
They flung it over the plain,
And all over Milton and Dorchester too
Great lumps of pudding the giants threw,
They tumbled as thick as rain.

Giant and mammoth have passed away,.
For ages have floated by;
The suet is hard as a marrow-bone,
And every plum is turned to a stone,
But there the puddings lie.

And if, some pleasant afternoon,
You'll ask me out to ride,
The whole of the story I will tell,
And you shall see where the puddings fell,
And pay for the punch beside.
        (Condensed.) Oliver Wendell Holmes.

THE FAIRIES OF THE CALDON-LOW

"AND where have you been, my Mary,
   And where have you been from me?"
"I've been to the top of the Caldon-Low,
   The midsummer night to see!"

"And what did you see, my Mary,
   All up on the Caldon-Low?"
"I saw the blithe sunshine come down,
   And I saw the merry winds blow."

"And what did you hear, my Mary,
   All up on the Caldon Hill?"
"I heard the drops of water made,
   And I heard the corn-ears fill."

"Oh tell me all, my Mary —
   All, all that ever you know;
For you must have seen the Fairies
   Last night on the Caldon-Low."

"Then take me on your knee, mother,
    And listen, mother of mine:
A hundred Fairies danced last night,
    And the harpers they were nine;

"And merry was the glee of the harp-strings,
    And their dancing feet so small;
But oh! the sound of their talking
    Was merrier far than all!"

"And what were the words, my Mary,
    That you did hear them say?"
"I'll tell you all, my mother,
    But let me have my way.

"And some they played with the water
    And rolled it down the hill;
'And this,' they said, 'shall speedily turn
    The poor old miller's mill;

"'For there has been no water
    Ever since the first of May;
And a busy man shall the miller be
    By the dawning of the day!

"'Oh the miller, how he will laugh,
    When he sees the mill-dam rise!
The jolly old miller, how he will laugh,
    Till the tears fill both his eyes!'

"And some they seized the little winds,
    That sounded over the hill,
And each put a horn into his mouth,
    And blew so sharp and shrill!

"'And there,' said they, 'the merry winds go
    Away from every horn;
And those shall clear the mildew dank
    From the blind old widow's corn:

"'Oh, the poor blind widow —
    Though she has been blind so long,
She'll be merry enough when the mildew's
        gone,
    And the corn stands stiff and strong!'

"And some they brought the brown linseed,
    And flung it down from the Low:
'And this,' said they, 'by the sunrise,
    In the weaver's croft shall grow!

"'Oh, the poor lame weaver!
    How will he laugh outright
When he sees his dwindling flax-field
    All full of flowers by night!'

"And then upspoke a Brownie,
    With a long beard on his chin;
'I have spun up all the tow,' said he,
    'And I want some more to spin.

“‘I’ve spun a piece of hempen cloth,
  And I want to spin another —
A little sheet for Mary’s bed
  And an apron for her mother!’

“And with that I could not help but laugh,
  And I laughed out loud and free;
And then on the top of the Caldon-Low,
  There was no one left but me.

“And all on the top of the Caldon-Low
  The mists were cold and gray,
And nothing I saw but the mossy stones
  That round about me lay.

“But, as I came down from the hill-top,
  I heard, afar below,
How busy the jolly miller was,
  And how merry the wheel did go!

“And I peeped into the widow’s field,
  And, sure enough, was seen
The yellow ears of the mildewed corn
  All standing stiff and green!

“And down by the weaver’s croft I stole,
  To see if the flax were high;
But I saw the weaver at his gate
  With the good news in his eye!

"Now, this is all that I heard, mother,
  And all that I did see;
So, prithee, make my bed, mother,
  For I'm tired as I can be!"
                                    Mary Howitt.

THE FAIRY FOLK

Up the airy mountain,
  Down the rushy glen,
We dare n't go a-hunting
  For fear of little men;
Wee folk, good folk,
  Trooping all together;
Green jacket, red cap,
  And white owl's feather!

Down along the rocky shore
  Some make their home,
They live on crispy pancakes
  Of yellow tide-foam;
Some in the reeds
  Of the black mountain-lake,
With frogs for their watch-dogs,
  All night awake.

High on the hill-top
  The old King sits;
He is now so old and gray
  He's nigh lost his wits.

With a bridge of white mist
  Columbkill he crosses,
On his stately journeys
  From Slieveleague to Rosses;
Or going up with music,
  On cold starry nights,
To sup with the Queen
  Of the gay Northern Lights.

They stole little Bridget
  For seven years long;
When she came down again
  Her friends were all gone.
They took her lightly back,
  Between the night and morrow;
They thought that she was fast asleep,
  But she was dead with sorrow.
They have kept her ever since
  Deep within the lakes,
On a bed of flag leaves,
  Watching till she wakes.

By the craggy hillside,
  Through the mosses bare,
They have planted thorn-trees
  For pleasure here and there.
Is any man so daring
  As dig one up in spite?

He shall find their sharpest thorns
  In his bed at night.

Up the airy mountain,
  Down the rushy glen,
We dare n't go a-hunting
  For fear of little men;
Wee folk, good folk,
  Trooping all together;
Green jacket, red cap,
  And white owl's feather.
William Allingham.

THE FAIRY QUEEN

Come, follow, follow me,
You, Fairy Elves that be;
Which circle on the greene,
  Come, follow Mab your Queene.
Hand in hand let's dance around,
For this place is fairye ground.

When mortals are at rest,
And snoring in their nest:
Unheard, and unespy'd,
  Through key-holes we do glide;
Over tables, stools, and shelves,
We trip it with our Fairy Elves.

And, if the house be foul
With platter, dish, or bowl,
Up stairs we nimbly creep,
And find the sluts asleep:
There we pinch their armes and thighes:
None escapes, nor none espies.

But if the house be swept,
And from uncleaness kept,
We praise the household maid,
And duely she is paid:
For we use before we goe
To drop a tester in her shoe.

Upon a mushroome's head
Our table-cloth we spread;
A grain of rye, or wheat,
Is manchet, which we eat;
Pearly drops of dew we drink
In acorn cups fill'd to the brink.

The brains of nightingales,
With unctuous fat of snailes,
Between two cockles stew'd,
Is meat that's easily chew'd;
Tailes of wormes, and marrow of mice,
Do make a dish, that's wonderous nice.

The grasshopper, gnat, and fly,
Serve for our minstrelsie;
Grace said, we dance a while,
And so the time beguile:
And if the moon doth hide her head,
The gloe-worm lights us home to bed.

On tops of dewie grasse
So nimbly do we passe,
The young and tender stalk
Ne'er bends when we do walk:
Yet in the morning may be seen
Where we the night before have been.

From Percy's Reliques of Ancient English Poetry.

THE FAIRY BOY

Part I

THE Laird of Co has left his hall,
And stands alone on the castle wall, —
His castle that hangs o'er the ocean-waves,
And rests on the roofs of the Fairy Caves.
Oh, sad and pensive there he stands,
Though his eye sees nought but his own broad
    lands,
Or far or near where his glance may go —
And keen is the glance of the Laird of Co!

"A fond farewell, ye scenes so dear,
A long, a last farewell, I fear,
For a boding voice seems whispering me,
'You never more these scenes shall see.'
But a tyrant's foot must now be stayed,
And my King has asked my sword in aid;
So fare-ye-well, 'tide weal or woe,
'Tide life or death, to the Laird of Co!"

Now rests his eye on the pennon gay
Of a bark that rides in the open bay,
And spreads before the freshening gale
The swelling breast of her snowy sail;
While youthful squire and stalwart knight,
With helm and corselet glancing bright,
Along her decks impatient go —
"You tarry long, O Laird of Co!"

"That comrades brave for me should wait!"
He quickly gains the castle-gate,
But there a boy before him stands,
A tiny cup in his tiny hands.
"My mother dear is weak and old,
Our home is dark, her couch is cold;
One cup of wine on her bestow
For charity, O Laird of Co!"

"Has never yet with will of mine
Unheeded been such prayer as thine.

Ho! Steward, take the boy with thee
And fill his cup for charity.
For charity? Poor child, I pray
When from such tale I turn away,
I dwell in home as dark and low
As thine, that now am Laird of Co!"

With rapid step he bends his way
To where the bark rides in the bay,
Her decks with arms and armor piled,
When comes the Steward, staring wild.
"That urchin strange — his elf-made cup
A butt of wine hath swallowed up!
Yet not a drop doth in it show —
Some fiend he is, O Laird of Co!"

"Or fiend or fairy, sprite or child,
Good Steward, let his cup be filled,
If wine enough of mine there be,
For well you know my word hath he:
Aye, every drop into it pour,
Till drained be every vault and store;
Pour till his beaker overflow —
Broke never his word a Laird of Co!"

Now back again the Steward hies,
And views the cup with wondering eyes,
While trembles every joint and limb —
One drop has filled it to the brim!

The boy departing softly said:
"When he on clay-cold couch is laid,
In home like mine, as dark and low,
I will repay the Laird of Co."

Part II

Oh, many a summer sun has shone,
And many a winter blast has blown,
Since sailed to foreign wars away
The bark that rode in the open bay!
And they who were but children then
Are women grown and bearded men,
And the old are gone where all must go
But comes not home the Laird of Co.

In cell where sunlight never falls,
And the damp runs down the blackened walls,
And slowly, darkly tracks its way
'Mong rotting straw on the floor of clay,
And rusts the fetters strongly bound
Around the captive on the ground,
So wan from suffering and woe —
Is this the comely Laird of Co!

"A soldier's death and soldier's grave,
On battle-field with comrades brave,
With lightsome heart I freely dared,
Nor of them thought, nor for them cared;

But thus, like felon vile, to lie
In hopeless, blank captivity,
In dungeon dark and damp and low —
And I was once the Laird of Co!"

What light, what light, like noontide clear,
Illumes the dungeon dark and drear?
What hand the door flings open wide,
As bar and lock-bolts backward glide?
A child beside the captive stands,
His bosom crossed with folded hands:
"I come to pay the debt I owe.
Arise, arise, poor Laird of Co!

"Arise, for thou art free again —"
His hand but touched the captive's chain,
And link and loop and lock and all
Like frost-nipped leaves in Autumn fall:
And strong and stalwart under him
Becomes each shrunken, wasted limb,
And he steps as stept he long ago,
When he went to the wars, the Laird of Co!

They mount the steep and winding stair,
Where dust makes thick the scanty air;
And through the gates that open stand
They pass unchallenged, hand in hand.
The boy's bright eyes are fixed on high —
His right hand pointed to the sky —

His foot he strikes on the earth below: —
"Now mount with me, O Laird of Co!"

Then up, up, up, to the starry sky!
They cleave the air that rushes by;
And on and on o'er wood and lea,
O'er lake and river, shore and sea;
While hamlets small and cities vast,
With blended lights go glancing past,
And fade away in the gloom below —
Where journeys he, the Laird of Co?

On earth again, and hand in hand
Before a castle's gate they stand —
A castle that hangs o'er the ocean-waves,
And rests on the roofs of the Fairy Caves.
"Farewell, I thus the wine repay
You gave for blessèd charity,
And your word held sacred long ago,
Farewell, farewell, good Laird of Co!"

From The Fairy Family.

THE PIED PIPER OF HAMELIN

I

HAMELIN town 's in Brunswick,
  By famous Hanover city;
The River Weser, deep and wide,
Washes its walls on the southern side;

A pleasanter spot you never spied;
  But, when begins my ditty,
Almost five hundred years ago,
To see the townsfolk suffer so
  From vermin, was a pity.

II

Rats!
They fought the dogs and killed the cats,
  And bit the babies in the cradles,
And ate the cheeses out of the vats,
  And licked the soup from the cooks' **own**
      ladles,
Split open the kegs of salted sprats,
Made nests inside men's Sunday hats,
And even spoiled the women's chats,
  By drowning their speaking
  With shrieking and squeaking
In fifty different sharps and flats.

III

At last the people in a body
  To the Town Hall came flocking;
"'T is clear," cried they, "our Mayor's **a**
      noddy,
  And as for our Corporation — shocking
To think we buy gowns lined with ermine
For dolts that can't or won't determine
What's best to rid us of our vermin!

You hope, because you're old and obese,
To find in the furry civic robe ease?
Rouse up, Sirs! Give your brains a racking
To find the remedy we're lacking,
Or, sure as fate, we'll send you packing!"
At this the Mayor and Corporation
Quaked with a mighty consternation.

IV

An hour they sate in Council;
At length the Mayor broke silence:
"For a guilder I'd my ermine gown sell;
I wish I were a mile hence!
It's easy to bid one rack one's brain —
I'm sure my poor head aches again,
I've scratched it so, and all in vain.
Oh, for a trap, a trap, a trap!"
Just as he said this, what should hap
At the chamber door, but a gentle tap.
"Bless us!" cried the Mayor, "what's that?"
(With the Corporation as he sat,
Looking little though wondrous fat;
Nor brighter was his eye, nor moister
Than a too-long-opened oyster,
Save when at noon his paunch grew mutinous
For a plate of turtle green and glutinous.)
"Only a scraping of shoes on the mat?
Anything like the sound of a rat
Makes my heart go pit-a-pat!"

V

"Come in!" the Mayor cried, looking bigger,
And in did come the strangest figure!
His queer long coat, from heel to head
Was half of yellow and half of red;
And he himself was tall and thin,
With sharp blue eyes, each like a pin,
And light loose hair, yet swarthy skin,
No tuft on cheek nor beard on chin,
But lips where smiles went out and in;
There was no guessing his kith and kin;
And nobody could enough admire
The tall man and his quaint attire.
Quoth one: "It's as if my great-grandsire,
Starting up at the trump of Doom's tone,
Had walked this way from his painted tomb-
    stone!"

VI

He advanced to the council table:
And, "Please your honours," said he, "I'm
    able,
By means of a secret charm, to draw
All creatures living beneath the sun,
That creep, or swim, or fly, or run,
After me so as you never saw!
And I chiefly use my charm
On creatures that do people harm, —
The mole, the toad, the newt, the viper:

And people call me the Pied Piper."
(And here they noticed round his neck
A scarf of red and yellow stripe
To match his coat of the self-same cheque;
And at the scarf's end hung a pipe;
And his fingers, they noticed, were ever
     straying
As if impatient to be playing
Upon his pipe, as low it dangled
Over his vesture so old-fangled.)
"Yet," said he, "poor piper as I am,
In Tartary I freed the Cham,
Last June, from his huge swarms of gnats;
I eased in Asia the Nizam
Of a monstrous brood of vampire-bats:
And as for what your brain bewilders,
If I can rid your town of rats
Will you give me a thousand guilders?"
"One? fifty thousand!" was the exclamation
Of the astonished Mayor and Corporation.

VII

Into the street the Piper stept,
   Smiling first a little smile,
As if he knew what magic slept
   In his quiet pipe the while;
Then, like a musical adept,
To blow the pipe his lips he wrinkled,
And green and blue his sharp eyes twinkled,

Like a candle-flame where salt is sprinkled;
And ere three shrill notes the pipe had uttered,
You heard as if an army muttered;
And the muttering grew to a grumbling;
And the grumbling grew to a mighty rum-
        bling;
And out of the houses the rats came tumbling.
Great rats, small rats, lean rats, brawny rats,
Brown rats, black rats, grey rats, tawny rats,
Grave old plodders, gay young friskers,
    Fathers, mothers, uncles, cousins,
Cocking tails, and pricking whiskers,
    Families by tens and dozens,
Brothers, sisters, husbands, wives —
Followed the Piper for their lives.
From street to street he piped, advancing,
And step for step they followed dancing,
Until they came to the River Weser,
Wherein all plunged and perished!
— Save one, who, stout as Julius Cæsar,
Swam across and lived to carry
(As he, the manuscript he cherished)
To Rat-land home his commentary:
Which was, "At the first shrill notes of the pipe
I heard a sound as of scraping tripe,
And putting apples, wondrous ripe,
Into a cider-press's gripe:
And a moving away of pickle-tub boards,
And a leaving ajar of conserve-cupboards,

And a drawing the corks of train-oil-flasks,
And a breaking the hoops of butter-casks:
And it seemed as if a voice
(Sweeter far than by harp or by psaltery
Is breathed) called out: 'Oh rats, rejoice!
The world is grown to one vast drysaltery!
So munch on, crunch on, take your nuncheon,
Breakfast, supper, dinner, luncheon!'
And just as a bulky sugar-puncheon,
All ready staved, like a great sun shone
Glorious, scarce an inch before me,
Just as methought it said, 'Come, bore me!'
— I found the Weser rolling o'er me."

VIII

You should have heard the Hamelin people
Ringing the bells till they rocked the steeple.
"Go," cried the Mayor, "and get long poles,
Poke out the nests, and block up the holes!
Consult with carpenters and builders,
And leave in our town not even a trace
Of the rats!" When suddenly, up the face
Of the Piper perked in the market-place,
With a, "First, if you please, my thousand
    guilders!"

IX

A thousand guilders! The Mayor looked blue;
So did the Corporation, too.

For council dinners made rare havoc
With Claret, Moselle, Vin-de-Grave, Hock;
And half the money would replenish
Their cellar's biggest butt with Rhenish.
To pay this sum to a wandering fellow,
With a gypsy coat of red and yellow!
"Beside," quoth the Mayor, with a knowing
        wink,
"Our business was done at the river's brink;
We saw with our eyes the vermin sink,
And what's dead can't come to life, I think.
So friend, we're not the folks to shrink
From the duty of giving you something for
        drink,
And a matter of money to put in your poke;
But as for the guilders, what we spoke
Of them, as you very well know, was in joke.
Beside, our losses have made us thrifty.
A thousand guilders! Come, take fifty!"

x

The Piper's face fell, and he cried:
"No trifling! I can't wait, beside!
I've promised to visit by dinner-time
Bagdad, and accept the prime
Of the Head-Cook's pottage, all he's rich in,
For having left, in the Caliph's kitchen,
Of a nest of scorpions no survivor.
With him I proved no bargain-driver;

With you, don't think I'll bate a stiver!
And folks who put me in a passion
May find me pipe after another fashion."

XI

"How!" cried the Mayor, "d'ye think I
    brook
Being worse treated than a Cook?
Insulted by a lazy ribald
With idle pipe and vesture piebald?
You threaten us, fellow? Do your worst;
Blow your pipe there till you burst!"

XII

Once more he stept into the street,
    And to his lips again
Laid his long pipe of smooth, straight cane;
    And ere he blew three notes (such sweet
Soft notes as yet musician's cunning
    Never gave the enraptured air)
There was a rustling that seemed like a
    bustling
Of merry crowds justling at pitching and
    hustling,
Small feet were pattering, wooden shoes clat-
    tering,
Little hands clapping and little tongues chat-
    tering,

And, like fowls in a farmyard when barley is
          scattering,
Out came the children running.
    And all the little boys and girls,
    With rosy cheeks and flaxen curls,
    And sparkling eyes and teeth like pearls,
Tripping and skipping ran merrily after
The wonderful music with shouting and
          laughter.

XIII

The Mayor was dumb, and the Council stood
As if they were changed into blocks of wood,
Unable to move a step, or cry
To the children merrily skipping by,
— Could only follow with the eye
That joyous crowd at the Piper's back.
And now the Mayor was on the rack,
And the wretched Council's bosoms beat,
As the Piper turned from the High Street
To where the Weser rolled its waters
Right in the way of their sons and daugh-
          ters!
However he turned from South to West,
And to Koppelberg Hill his steps addressed,
And after him the children pressed;
Great was the joy in every breast.
"He never can cross that mighty top!
He's forced to let the piping drop,

And we shall see our children stop!"
When, lo, as they reached the mountain-
    side,
A wondrous portal opened wide,
As if a cavern was suddenly hollowed;
And the Piper advanced, and the children
    followed,
And when all were in to the very last,
The door in the mountain-side shut fast.
Did I say all? No! One was lame,
And could not dance the whole of the way;
And in after years, if you would blame
His sadness, he was used to say: —
"It's dull in our town since my playmates
    left!
I can't forget that I'm bereft
Of all the pleasant sights they see,
Which the Piper also promised me:
For he led us, he said, to a joyous land,
Joining the town and just at hand,
Where waters gushed and fruit trees grew,
And flowers put forth a fairer hue,
And everything was strange and new;
The sparrows were brighter than peacocks
    here,
And their dogs outran our fallow-deer,
And honey-bees had lost their stings,
And horses were born with eagles' wings:
And just as I became assured

My lame foot would be speedily cured,
The music stopped, and I stood still,
And found myself outside the hill,
Left alone against my will,
To go now limping as before,
And never hear of that country more!"

XIV

Alas, alas for Hamelin!
   There came into many a burgher's pate
   A text which says that Heaven's gate
   Opes to the rich at as easy rate
As the needle's eye takes a camel in!
The Mayor sent East, West, North, and
     South,
To offer the Piper, by word of mouth,
   Wherever it was man's lot to find him,
Silver and gold to his heart's content,
If he'd only return the way he went,
   And bring the children behind him.
But when they saw 't was a lost endeavour,
And Piper and dancers were gone for ever,
They made a decree that lawyers never
   Should think their records dated duly
If, after the day of the month and the year,
These words did not as well appear,
"And so long after what happened here
   On the Twenty-second of July,
Thirteen hundred and seventy-six":

And the better in memory to fix
The place of the children's last retreat,
They called it, the Pied Piper's Street —
Where any one playing on pipe or tabor
Was sure for the future to lose his labour.
Nor suffered they hostelry or tavern
   To shock with mirth a street so solemn;
But opposite the place of the cavern
   They wrote the story on a column,
And on the great church-window painted
The same, to make the world acquainted
How their children were stolen away,
And there it stands to this very day.
And I must not omit to say
That in Transylvania there's a tribe
Of alien people that ascribe
The outlandish ways and dress
On which their neighbours lay such stress,
To their fathers and mothers having risen
Out of some subterraneous prison
Into which they were trepanned
Long ago in a mighty band
Out of Hamelin town in Brunswick land,
But how or why, they don't understand.

XV

So, Willy, let you and me be wipers
Of scores out with all men, — especially
     pipers!

And, whether they pipe us free from rats or
    from mice,
If we've promised them aught, let us keep
    our promise!

Robert Browning.

GOBLIN MARKET

Part I

MORNING and evening
Maids heard the Goblins cry:
"Come buy our orchard fruits,
Come buy, come buy!
Apples and quinces,
Lemons and oranges,
Plump unpecked cherries,
Melons and raspberries,
Bloom-down-cheeked peaches,
Swart-headed mulberries,
Wild free-born cranberries,
Crab-apples, dewberries,
Pine-apples, blackberries,
Apricots, strawberries;—
Taste them and try;
Currants and gooseberries,
Bright-fire-like barberries,
Figs to fill your mouth,
Citrons from the south,

Sweet to tongue and sound to eye;
Come buy, come buy!"
Evening by evening
Among the brookside rushes,
Laura bowed her head to hear,
Lizzie veiled her blushes;
Crouching close together
In the cooling weather,
With clasping arms and cautioning lips,
With tingling cheeks and finger tips.
"Lie close," Laura said,
Pricking up her golden head,
"We must not look at Goblin men,
We must not buy their fruits!
Who knows upon what soil they fed
Their hungry, thirsty roots?"

"Come buy," call the Goblins
Hobbling down the glen.
"Oh," cried Lizzie, "Laura, Laura,
You should not peep at Goblin men!"
Lizzie covered up her eyes,
Covered close lest they should look;
Laura reared her glossy head,
And whispered like the restless brook:
"Look, Lizzie, look, Lizzie,
Down the glen tramp little men.
One hauls a basket,
One bears a plate,

One lugs a golden dish
Of many pounds' weight.
How fair the vine must grow
Whose grapes are so luscious;
How warm the wind must blow
Through those fruit bushes!"
"No," said Lizzie, "No, no, no:
Their offers should not charm us,
Their evil gifts would harm us!"
She thrust a dimpled finger
In each ear, shut eyes and ran.

Curious Laura chose to linger
Wondering at each merchant man.
One had a cat's face,
One whisked a tail,
One tramped at a rat's pace,
One crawled like a snail.
When they reached where Laura was
They stood stock still upon the moss.
One set his basket down,
One reared his plate;
One began to weave a crown
Of tendrils, leaves, and rough nuts brown;
One heaved the golden weight
Of dish and fruit to offer her:
"Come buy, come buy," was still their
      cry,
Laura stared but did not stir,

Longed but had no money.
The whisk-tailed merchant bade her taste
In tones as smooth as honey.

But sweet-tooth Laura spoke in haste:
"Good Folk, I have no coin;
To take were to purloin.
I have no copper in my purse,
I have no silver either,
And all my gold is on the furze
That shakes in windy weather
Above the rusty heather!"
"You have much gold upon your head,"
They answered all together,
"Buy from us with a golden curl."
She clipped a precious golden lock,
She dropped a tear more rare than pearl,
Then sucked their fruit-globes fair or red.
Sweeter than the honey from the rock,
Stronger than man-rejoicing wine,
Clearer than water flowed that juice;
She never tasted such before,
How should it cloy with length of use?
She sucked, and sucked, and sucked the
          more
Fruits which that unknown orchard bore;
She sucked until her lips were sore;
Then flung the emptied rinds away
But gathered up one kernel stone,

And knew not was it night or day
As she turned home alone.

Lizzie met her at the gate,
Full of wise upbraidings:
"Dear, you should not stay so late,
Twilight is not good for maidens;
Should not loiter in the glen
In the haunts of Goblin men.
Do you not remember Jeanie,
How she met them in the moonlight,
Took their gifts both choice and many,
Ate their fruits and wore their flowers
Plucked from bowers
Where summer ripens at all hours?
But ever in the moonlight
She pined and pined away;
Sought them by night and day,
Found them no more, but dwindled and
      grew grey;
Then fell with the first snow;
While to this day no grass will grow
Where she lies low:
I planted daisies there a year ago
That never blow.
You should not loiter so!"
"Nay, hush," said Laura,
"Nay, hush, my sister!
I ate and ate my fill,

Yet my mouth waters still!
To-morrow night I will
Buy more!" and kissed her.

Part II

Early in the morning
When the first cock crowed his warning,
Neat like bees, as sweet and busy,
Laura rose with Lizzie;
Fetched in honey, milked the cows,
Aired and set to rights the house,
Kneaded cakes of whitest wheat,
Cakes for dainty mouths to eat,
Next churned butter, whipped up cream,
Fed their poultry, sat and sewed;
Talked as modest maidens should;
Lizzie with an open heart,
Laura in an absent dream,
One content, one sick in part;
One warbling for the mere bright day's
    delight,
One longing for the night.

At length slow evening came.
They went with pitchers to the reedy
    brook;
Lizzie most placid in her look,
Laura most like a leaping flame.

They drew the gurgling water from its
        deep.
Lizzie plucked purple and rich golden
        flags,
Then turning homeward said: "The sun-
        set flushes
Those furthest loftiest crags;
Come, Laura, not another maiden lags.
No wilful squirrel wags,
The beasts and birds are fast asleep."
But Laura loitered still among the rushes,
And said the bank was steep,
And said the hour was early still,
The dew not fallen, the wind not chill;
Listening ever, but not catching
The customary cry:
"Come buy, come buy!"
Till Lizzie urged: "O Laura, come;
I hear the fruit-call, but I dare not look.
You should not loiter longer at this brook,
Come with me home."
Laura turned cold as stone
To find her sister heard that cry alone,
That Goblin cry,
"Come buy our fruits, come buy!"
. . . .

Day after day, night after night,
Laura kept watch in vain,
In sullen silence of exceeding pain.

She never caught again the Goblin cry:
"Come buy, come buy!"
She never spied the Goblin men
Hawking their fruits along the glen;
But when the noon waxed bright
Her hair grew thin and grey;
She dwindled, as the fair full moon doth
         turn
To swift decay and burn
Her fire away!
She no more swept the house,
Tended the fowls or cows,
Fetched honey, kneaded cakes of wheat,
Brought water from the brook;
But sat down listless in the chimney-nook
And would not eat.

Tender Lizzie could not bear
To watch her sister's cankerous care,
Yet not to share.
She night and morning
Caught the Goblin's cry:
"Come buy our orchard fruits,
Come buy, come buy!"
Beside the brook, along the glen,
She heard the tramp of Goblin men, —
The voice and stir
Poor Laura could not hear, —
Longed to buy fruit to comfort her,

But feared to pay too dear;
Till Laura dwindling
Seemed knocking at Death's door.
Then Lizzie weighed no more
Better and worse;
But put a silver penny in her purse.
Kissed Laura, crossed the heath with
    clumps of furze,
At twilight, halted by the brook;
And for the first time in her life
Began to listen and look!

Laughed every Goblin
When they spied her peeping;
Came towards her hobbling,
Flying, running, leaping,
Puffing, and blowing,
Chuckling, clapping, crowing,
Clucking, and gobbling,
Mopping, and mowing,
Full of airs and graces,
Pulling wry faces,
Demure grimaces,
Hugged her and kissed her;
Squeezed and caressed her;
Stretched up their dishes,
Panniers, and plates:
"Look at our apples
Russet and dun,

Bob at our cherries,
Bite at our peaches,
Citrons and dates,
Grapes for the asking,
Pears red with basking
Out in the sun,
Plums on their twigs;
Pluck them and suck them, —
Pomegranates, figs!"
"Good Folk," said Lizzie,
Mindful of Jeanie,
"Give me much and many."
Held out her apron,
Tossed them her penny.
"Nay, take a seat with us,
Honor and eat with us,"
They answered grinning: —
"Our feast is but beginning.
Night yet is early,
Warm and dew-pearly,
Wakeful and starry;
Such fruits as these
No man can carry;
Half their bloom would fly,
Half their dew would dry,
Half their flavor would pass **by.**
Sit down and feast with us,
Be welcome guest with us,
Cheer you and rest with us!"

"Thank you," said Lizzie, "But one waits
At home alone for me;
So without further parleying,
If you will not sell me any
Of your fruits though much and many
Give me back my silver penny
I tossed you for a fee." —
They began to scratch their pates,
No longer wagging, purring,
But visibly demurring,
Grunting and snarling. —
One called her proud,
Cross-grained, uncivil;
Their tones waxed loud,
Their looks were evil.
Lashing their tails
They trod and hustled her,
Elbowed and jostled her,
Twitched her hair out by the roots,
Stamped upon her tender feet,
Held her hands and squeezed their fruits
Against her mouth to make her eat.

One may lead a horse to water,
Twenty cannot make him drink.
Though the Goblins cuffed and caught
      her,
Coaxed and fought her,
Bullied and besought her,

Scratched her, pinched her black as ink,
Kicked and knocked her,
Mauled and mocked her,
Lizzie uttered not a word;
Would not open lip from lip
Lest they should cram a mouthful in;
But laughed in heart to feel the drip
Of juice that syruped all her face,
And lodged in dimples of her chin,
And streaked her neck which quaked like
      curd.
At last the evil people,
Worn out by her resistance,
Flung back her penny,
Kicked their fruit,
Along whichever road they took,
Not leaving root or stone or shoot;
Some writhed into the ground,
Some dived into the brook
With ring and ripple,
Some scudded on the gale without a
      sound,
Some vanished in the distance.

In a smart, ache, tingle,
Lizzie went her way;
Knew not was it night or day;
Sprang up the bank, tore thro' the furze,
Threaded copse and dingle,

And heard her penny jingle
Bouncing in her purse. —
She cried: "Laura," up the garden,
"Did you miss me?
Come and kiss me!
Never mind my bruises,
Hug me, kiss me, suck my juices
Squeezed from Goblin fruits for you,
Goblin pulp and Goblin dew!
Eat me, drink me, love me;
Laura, make much of me;
For your sake I have braved the glen,
And had to do with Goblin merchant
      men!"

Laura started from her chair,
Flung her arms up in the air,
Clutched her hair:
"Lizzie, Lizzie, have you tasted
For my sake the fruit forbidden?
Must your light like mine be hidden,
Your young life like mine be wasted,
Undone in mine undoing,
And ruined in my ruin,
Thirsty, cankered, Goblin-ridden?" —
She clung about her sister,
Kissed and kissed and kissed her.
Her lips began to scorch,
That juice was wormwood to her tongue,

She loathed the feast;
Writhing as one possessed she leaped
            and sung,
Rent all her robe, and wrung
Her hands in lamentable haste,
And beat her breast!
Like a lightning-stricken mast,
Like a wind-uprooted tree
Spun about,
Like a foam-topped waterspout
Cast down headlong in the sea,
She fell at last;
Pleasure past, and anguish past,
Is it death or is it life?

Life out of death.
That night long, Lizzie watched by
            her,
Counted her pulse's flagging stir,
Felt for her breath,
Held water to her lips, and cooled her
            face
With tears and fanning leaves.
But when the first birds chirped about
            their eaves,
And early reapers plodded to the
            place
Of golden sheaves,
And dew-wet grass,

Bowed in the morning winds so brisk to
        pass,
And new buds with new day
Opened of cup-like lilies on the stream,
Laura awoke as from a dream,
Laughed in the innocent old way,
Hugged Lizzie but not twice or thrice;
Her gleaming locks showed not one
        thread of grey,
Her breath was sweet as May,
And light danced in her eyes.

(Condensed.) Christina Rossetti.

THE BROWN DWARF OF RÜGEN

THE pleasant isle of Rügen looks the Baltic
        water o'er,
To the silver sanded beaches of the Pomera-
        nian shore;

And in the town of Rambin a little boy and
        maid
Plucked the meadow-flowers together and in
        the sea-surf played.

Alike were they in beauty if not in their
        degree:
He was the Amptman's first-born, the miller's
        child was she.

Now of old the isle of Rügen was full of
    Dwarfs and Trolls,
The brown-faced little Earth-men, the people
    without souls;

And for every man and woman in Rügen's
    island found
Walking in air and sunshine, a Troll was
    underground.

It chanced the little maiden, one morning,
    strolled away
Among the haunted Nine Hills, where the
    Elves and Goblins play.

That day, in barley fields below, the harvest-
    ers had known
Of evil voices in the air, and heard the small
    horns blown.

She came not back; the search for her in field
    and wood was vain:
They cried her east, they cried her west, but
    she came not again.

"She's down among the Brown Dwarfs,"
    said the dream-wives wise and old,
And prayers were made, and masses said, and
    Rambin's church bell tolled.

Five years her father mourned her; and then
    John Deitrich said:
"I will find my little playmate, be she alive
    or dead."

He watched among the Nine Hills, he heard
    the Brown Dwarfs sing,
And saw them dance by moonlight merrily
    in a ring.

And when their gay-robed leader tossed up
    his cap of red,
Young Deitrich caught it as it fell, and thrust
    it on his head.

The Troll came crouching at his feet and wept
    for lack of it.
"Oh, give me back my magic cap, for your
    great head unfit!"

"Nay," Deitrich said, "the Dwarf who throws
    his charmèd cap away,
Must serve its finder at his will, and for his
    folly pay.

"You stole my pretty Lisbeth, and hid her in
    the earth;
And you shall ope the door of glass and let
    me lead her forth."

"She will not come; she's one of us; she's
    mine!" the Brown Dwarf said,
"The day is set, the cake is baked, to-morrow
    we shall wed."

"The fell fiend fetch thee!" Deitrich cried,
    "and keep thy foul tongue still.
Quick! open to thy evil world, the glass door
    of the hill!"

The Dwarf obeyed; and youth and Troll down
    the long stairway passed,
And saw in dim and sunless light a country
    strange and vast.

Weird, rich, and wonderful, he saw the Elfin
    under-land, —
Its palaces of precious stones, its streets of
    golden sand.

He came into a banquet-hall with tables
    richly spread,
Where a young maiden served to him the red
    wine and the bread.

How fair she seemed among the Trolls so
    ugly and so wild!
Yet pale and very sorrowful, like one who
    never smiled!

Her low, sweet voice, her gold-brown hair,
    her tender blue eyes seemed
Like something he had seen elsewhere or
    something he had dreamed.

He looked; he clasped her in his arms; he knew
    the long-lost one:
"O Lisbeth! See thy playmate — I am the
    Amptman's son!"

She leaned her fair head on his breast, and
    through her sobs she spoke:
"Oh, take me from this evil place, and from
    the Elfin folk!

"And let me tread the grass-green fields and
    smell the flowers again,
And feel the soft wind on my cheek and hear
    the dropping rain!

"And oh, to hear the singing bird, the rustling
    of the tree,
The lowing cows, the bleat of sheep, the
    voices of the sea;

"And oh, upon my father's knee to sit beside
    the door,
And hear the bell of vespers ring in Rambin
    church once more!"

He kissed her cheek, he kissed her lips; the
    Brown Dwarf groaned to see:
And tore his tangled hair and ground his long
    teeth angrily.

But Deitrich said: "For five long years this
    tender Christian maid
Has served you in your evil world, and well
    must she be paid!

"Haste! — hither bring me precious gems,
    the richest in your store;
Then when we pass the gate of glass, you'll
    take your cap once more."

No choice was left the baffled Troll, and, mur-
    muring, he obeyed,
And filled the pockets of the youth and apron
    of the maid.

They left the dreadful under-land and passed
    the gate of glass;
They felt the sunshine's warm caress, they
    trod the soft, green grass.

And when, beneath, they saw the Dwarf
    stretch up to them his brown
And crooked claw-like fingers, they tossed his
    red cap down.

Oh, never shone so bright a sun, was never
    sky so blue,
As hand in hand they homeward walked the
    pleasant meadows through!

And never sang the birds so sweet in Rambin's
    woods before,
And never washed the waves so soft along the
    Baltic shore;

And when beneath his door-yard trees the
    father met his child,
The bells rung out their merriest peal, the
    folks with joy ran wild.

And soon from Rambin's holy church the
    twain came forth as one,
The Amptman kissed a daughter, the miller
    blest a son.

John Deitrich's fame went far and wide, and
    nurse and maid crooned o'er
Their cradle song: "Sleep on, sleep well, the
    Trolls shall come no more!"

For in the haunted Nine Hills he set a cross
    of stone;
And Elf and Brown Dwarf sought in vain a
    door where door was none.

The tower he built in Rambïn, fair Rügen's
    pride and boast,
Looked o'er the Baltic water to the Pome-
    ranian coast;

And, for his worth ennobled, and rich beyond
    compare,
Count Deitrich and his lovely bride dwelt
    long and happy there.

John Greenleaf Whittier.

THE WORME OF LAMBTON

The Sinning

IT is the joyful Easter morn,
    And the bells ring loud and clear,
Sounding the holy day of rest
    Through the quiet vale of Wear.

And buxom youth and bashful maid,
    In holiday array,
Thro' verdant glade and greenwood shade,
    To Brigford bend their way.

And soon within its sacred dome
    Their wandering steps are stayed;
The bell is rung, the mass is sung,
    And the solemn prayer is prayed.

But why did Lambton's youthful heir
  Not mingle with the throng?
And why did he not bend his knee,
  Nor join in the holy song?

O Lambton's heir is a wicked man!
  Alike in word and deed;
He makes a jest of psalm and priest,
  Of the Ave and the Creed.

And Lambton's heir, at the matin prayer,
  Or the vesper, is not seen;
And on this day of rest and peace
  He hath donned his coat of green;

And with his creel slung on his back,
  His light rod in his hand,
Down by the side of the shady Wear
  He took his lonely stand.

There was no sound but the rushing stream,
  The little birds were still,
As if they knew that Lambton's heir
  Was doing a deed of ill.

He threw his line, of the costly twine,
  Across the gentle stream;
Upon its top the dun-flies drop
  Lightly as childhood's dream.

Again, again, — but all in vain,
  In the shallow or the deep;
No trout rose to his cunning bait;
  He heard no salmon leap.

And now he wandered east the stream,
  And now he wandered west;
He sought each bank or hanging bush,
  Which fishes love the best.

But vain was all his skilful art;
  Vain was each deep disguise;
Vain was alike the varied bait,
  And vain the mimic flies.

The Worme

When tired and vexed, the castle bell
  Rung out the hour of dine,
"Now," said the Lambton's youthful heir,
  "A weary lot is mine!"

"For six long hours, this April morn,
  My line in vain I've cast;
But one more throw; come weal come woe,
  For this shall be the last!"

He took from his bag a maggot worm,
  That bait of high renown;
His line wheeled quickly through the air,
  Then sunk in the water down.

When he drew it out, his ready hand
  With no quivering motion shook,
For neither salmon, trout nor ged,
  Had fastened on his hook;

But a little thing, *a strange formed thing,*
  Like a piece of muddy weed;
But like no fish that swims the stream,
  Nor aught that crawls the mead.

'T was scarce an inch and a half in length,
  Its color the darkest green;
And on its rough and scaly back
  Two little fins were seen.

It had a long and pointed snout,
  Like the mouth of the slimy eel,
And its white and loosely hanging jaws
  Twelve pin-like teeth reveal.

It had sharp claws upon its feet,
  Short ears upon its head,
A jointed tail, and quick bright eyes,
  That gleamed of a fiery red.

"Art thou the prize," said the weary wight,
  "For which I have spent my time;
For which I have toiled till the hour of noon,
  Since rang the matin chime!"

From the side of the dell, a crystal well
  Sends its waters bubbling by;
"Rest there, thou ugly tiny elf,
  Either to live or die!"

He threw it in, and when next he came,
  He saw, to his surprise,
It was a foot and a half in length;
  It had grown so much in size.
And its wings were long, far-stretched and strong,
  And redder were its eyes!

The Curse

But Lambton's heir is an altered man, —
  At the church on bended knee,
Three times a day he was wont to pray; —
  And now he's beyond the sea.

He has done penance for his sins,
  He has drank of a sainted well,
He has joined the band from the Holy Land
  To chase the infidel.

Where host met host, and strife raged most,
  His sword flashed high and bright;
Where force met force, he winged his course,
  The foremost in the fight.

Pure was his fame, unstained his shield;
  A merciful man was he;

The friend of the weak, he raised not his hand
    'Gainst a fallen enemy.

Thus on the plains of Palestine,
    He gained a mighty name,
And, full of honor and renown,
    To the home of his childhood came.

But when he came to his father's lands,
    No cattle were grazing there;
The grass in the mead was unmown and rough,
    And the fields untilled and bare.

And when he came to his father's hall,
    He wondered what might ail;
His sire but coolly welcomed him,
    And his sister's cheeks were pale.

"Now why, now why, this frozen cheer?
    What is it that may ail?
Why tremble thus my father dear?
    My sister, why so pale?"

"O! sad and woful has been our lot,
    Whilst thou wast far away;
For a mighty Dragon hath hither come
    And taken up its stay;
At night or morn it sleepeth not,
    But watcheth for its prey.

"'T is ten cloth yards in length; its hue
  Is of the darkest green,
And on its rough and scaly back,
  Two strong black wings are seen.

"It hath a long and pointed snout,
  Like the mighty crocodile;
And, from its grinning jaws, stand out
  Its teeth in horrid file.

"It hath on each round and webbed foot
  Four sharp and hooked claws;
And its jointed tail, with heavy trail,
  Over the ground it draws.

"It hath two rough and hairy ears
  Upon its bony head;
Its eyes shine like the winter sun,
  Fearful, and darkly red.

"Its roar is loud as the thunder's sound,
  But shorter and more shrill;
It rolls, with many a heavy bound,
  Onward from hill to hill.

"And each morn, *at the matin chime*,
  It seeks the lovely Wear;
And, at the noontide bell,
  It gorges its fill, then seeks the hill
Where springs the crystal well.

"No knight has e'er returned who dared
    The monster to assail.
Though he struck off an ear or limb,
    Or lopt its jointed tail,
Its severed limbs again unite,
    Strong as the iron mail.

"My horses and sheep, and all my kine,
    The ravenous beast hath killed;
With oxen and deer, from far and near,
    Its hungry maw is filled.
'T is hence the mead is unmown and long,
And the corn-fields are untilled!

"My son, to hail thee here in health,
    My very heart is glad;
But thou hast heard our tale — and say,
    Canst thou wonder that we're sad?"

The Witch of the Glen

And sorrowful was Lambton's heir;
    "My sinful act," said he,
"This curse hath on the country brought,
    Be it mine to set it free!"

Deep in the dell, in a ruined hut,
    Far from the homes of men,
There dwelt a witch the peasants called
    Old Elspat of the Glen.

'T was a dark night, and the stormy wind
  Howled with a hollow moan,
As through tangled copsewood, bush and
    briar,
  He sought the aged crone.

She sat on a low and three-legg'd stool,
  Beside a dying fire;
As he lifted the latch she stirred the brands,
  And the smoky flames blazed higher.

She was a woman weak and old,
  Her form was bent and thin;
And on her lean and shrivelled hand,
  She rested her pointed chin.

He entered with fear, that dauntless man,
  And spake of all his need;
He gave her gold; he asked her aid,
  How best he might succeed.

"Clothe thee," said she, "in armor bright,
  In mail of glittering sheen,
All studded o'er, behind and before,
  With razors sharp and keen;

"And take in thy hand the trusty brand
  Which thou bore beyond the sea;

And make to the Virgin a solemn vow,
    If she grant thee victory:
What meets thee first, when the strife is o'er,
    Her offering shall be."

The Dragon

He went to the fight, in armor bright,
    Equipped from head to heel;
His gorget closed, and his visor shut,
    He seemed a form of steel.

But with razor blades all sharp and keen,
    The mail was studded o'er;
And his long tried and trusty brand
    In his greaved hand he bore.

He made to the Virgin a solemn vow,
    If she granted victory,
What met him first on his homeward path
    Her sacrifice should be.

He told his sire, when he heard the horn,
    To slip his favorite hound;
"'T will quickly seek its master's side
    At the accustomed sound."

Forward he trod, with measured step,
    To meet his foe, alone,
While the first beams of the morning sun
    On his massy armor shone.

The monster slept on an island crag
  Lulled by the rustling Wear,
Which eddied turbid at the base
  Though elsewhere smooth and clear.

It lay in repose, its wings were flat,
  Its ears fell on its head,
Its legs stretched out, and drooped its snout,
  But its eyes were fiery red.

Little feared he, that armed knight,
  As he left the rocky shore;
And in his hand prepared for fight
  His unsheathed sword he bore.

As he plunged in, the water's splash
  The monster startling hears;
It spreads its wings, and the valley rings,
  Like the clash of a thousand spears.

It bristled up its scaly back,
  Curled high its jointed tail,
And ready stood with grinning teeth,
  The hero to assail.

Then sprung at the knight, with all its might,
  And its foamy teeth it gnashed;
With its jointed tail, like a thrasher's flail,
  The flinty rocks it lashed.

It rose on high, and darkened the sky,
  Then with a hideous yell,
A moment winnowed th' air with its wings,
  And down like a mountain fell.

He stood prepared for the falling blow,
  But mournful was his fate;
Awhile he reeled, then staggering, fell
  Beneath the monster's weight.

And round about its prostrate foe
  Its fearful length it rolled,
And clasped him close, till his armor cracked
  Within its scaly fold;

But pierced by the blades, from body and
      breast
  Fast did the red blood pour;
Cut by the blades, piece fell by piece
  And quivered in the gore.

Piece fell by piece, foot fell by foot;
  No more is the river clear,
But stained with blood as the severed limbs
  Rolled down the rushing Wear.

Piece fell by piece, and inch by inch,
  From the body and the tail;
But the head still hung by the gory teeth,
  Tight fastened in the mail.

It panted long, and fast it breathed,
   With many a bitter groan;
Its eyes grew dim, it loosed its hold,
   And fell like a lifeless stone!

The Fate of Lambton

Then loud he blew his bugle-horn,
   The blast of victory!
From rock to rock the sound was borne,
   By Echo, glad and free;
For, burdened long by the Dragon's roar,
   She joyed in her liberty!

But not his hound, with gladdened bound,
   Comes leaping at the call;
With feelings dire he sees *his sire*
   Rush from his ancient hall!

When Lambton's anxious listening Lord
   Heard the bugle-note so wild,
He thought no more of his plighted word,
   But ran to clasp his child!

"Strange is my lot," said the luckless wight,
   "How sorrow and joy combine!
When high in fame to my home I came,
   My kindred did weep and pine.

"This morn my triumph sees, and sees
  Dishonor light on me;
For I had vowed to the Holy Maid
  If she gave me victory,
What first I met, when the fight was o'er,
  Her offering should be!

" I thought to have slain my gallant hound,
  Beneath my unwilling knife;
But I cannot raise my hand on him
  Who gave my being life!"

And heavy and sorrowful was his heart,
  And he hath gone again
To seek advice of the wise woman,
  Old Elspat of the Glen.

"Since thy solemn vow is unfulfilled,
  Though greater be thy fame,
Thou must a lofty chapel build
  To the Virgin Mary's name.

"On nine generations of thy race,
  A heavy curse shall fall;
They may die in the fight or in the chase,
  But not in their native hall!"

He builded there a chapel fair,
  And rich endowment made,

Where morn and eve, by cowled monks
  In sable garb arrayed,
The bell was rung, the mass was sung,
  And the solemn prayer was made.

(Condensed.) J. Watson.

ST. GEORGE AND THE DRAGON

OF Hector's deeds did Homer sing,
  And of the sack of stately Troy,
What griefs fair Helena did bring,
  Which was Sir Paris's only joy;
And by my pen I will recite
St. George's deeds, an English knight.

Against the Sarazens so rude
  Fought he full long and many a day,
Where many giants he subdued,
  In honor of the Christian way;
And after many adventures past,
To Egypt land he came at last.

Now, as this story plain doth tell,
  Within that country there did rest
A dreadful Dragon fierce and fell,
  Whereby they were full sore oppressed;
Who by his poisonous breath each day
Did many of the city slay.

The grief whereof did grow so great
  Throughout the limits of the land,
That they their wise-men did entreat
  To show their cunning out of hand;
What way they might this fiend destroy,
That did the country thus annoy.

The wise-men all before the King,
  This answer fram'd incontinent:
The Dragon none to death might bring
  By any means they could invent;
His skin more hard than brass was found,
That sword nor spear could pierce nor wound.

When this the people understood,
  They cryed out most piteously,
The Dragon's breath infects their blood,
  That every day in heaps they die;
Among them such a plague it bred,
The living scarce could bury the dead.

No means there were, as they could hear,
  For to appease the Dragon's rage,
But to present some virgin clear,
  Whose blood his fury might assuage;
Each day he would a maiden eat,
For to allay his hunger great.

This thing by art the wise-men found,
  Which truly must observèd be;

Wherefore, throughout the city round,
  A virgin pure of good degree
Was, by the King's commission, still
Taken up to serve the Dragon's will.

Thus did the Dragon every day
  Untimely crop some virgin flower,
Till all the maids were worn away,
  And none were left him to devour;
Saving the King's fair daughter bright,
Her father's only heart's delight.

Then came the officers to the King,
  That heavy message to declare,
Which did his heart with sorrow sting;
  "She is," quoth he, "my kingdom's heir;
O let us all be poisoned here,
Ere she should die, that is my dear."

Then rose the people presently,
  And to the King in rage they went;
They said his daughter dear should die,
  The Dragon's fury to prevent:
"Our daughters all are dead," quoth they,
"And have been made the Dragon's prey;

And by their blood we rescued were,
  And thou hast saved thy life thereby;
And now in sooth it is but fair,
  For us thy daughter so should die."

"O save my daughter," said the King,
"And let me feel the Dragon's sting."

Then fell fair Sabra on her knee,
    And to her father dear did say:
"O father, strive not thus for me,
    But let me be the Dragon's prey;
It may be, for my sake alone
This plague upon the land was thrown."

"'T is better I should die," she said,
    "Than all your subjects perish quite;
Perhaps the Dragon here was laid,
    For my offence to work his spite,
And after he hath sucked my gore,
Your land shall feel the grief no more."

"What hast thou done, my daughter dear,
    For to deserve this heavy scourge?
It is my fault, as may appear,
    Which makes the gods our state to purge;
Then ought I die, to stint the strife,
And to preserve thy happy life."

Like mad-men, all the people cried:
    "Thy death to us can do no good;
Our safety only doth abide
    In making her the Dragon's food."
"Lo! here I am, I come," quoth she,
"Therefore do what you will with me."

"Nay stay, dear daughter," quoth the Queen,
  "And as thou art a virgin bright,
That hast for virtue famous been,
  So let me clothe thee all in white;
And crown thy head with flowers sweet,
An ornament for virgins meet."

And when she was attired so,
  According to her mother's mind,
Unto the stake then did she go,
  To which her tender limbs they bind;
And being bound to stake a thrall,
She bade farewell unto them all.

"Farewell, my father dear," quoth she,
  "And my sweet mother meek and mild;
Take you no thought nor weep for me,
  For you may have another child;
Since for my country's good I die,
Death I receive most willingly."

The King and Queen and all their train
  With weeping eyes went then their way,
And let their daughter there remain,
  To be the hungry Dragon's prey:
But as she did there weeping lie,
Behold St. George came riding by.

And seeing there a lady bright
  So rudely tied unto a stake,

As well became a valiant knight,
  He straight to her his way did take:
"Tell me, sweet maiden," then quoth he,
"What caitiff thus abuseth thee?

"And, lo! by Christ his cross I vow,
  Which here is figured on my breast,
I will revenge it on his brow,
  And break my lance upon his chest;"
And speaking thus whereas he stood,
The Dragon issued from the wood.

The lady, that did first espy
  The dreadful Dragon coming so,
Unto St. George aloud did cry,
  And willed him away to go;
"Here comes that cursed fiend," quoth she,
"That soon will make an end of me."

St. George then looking round about,
  The fiery Dragon soon espied,
And like a knight of courage stout,
  Against him did most furiously ride;
And with such blows he did him greet,
He fell beneath his horse's feet.

For with his lance that was so strong,
  As he came gaping in his face,
In at his mouth he thrust along;
  For he could pierce no other place:

And thus within the lady's view
This mighty Dragon straight he slew.

The savor of his poisoned breath
  Could do this holy knight no harm;
Thus he the lady saved from death,
  And home he led her by the arm;
Which when King Ptolemy did see,
There was great mirth and melody.

When as that valiant champion there
  Had slain the Dragon in the field,
To court he brought the lady fair,
  Which to their hearts much joy did yield,
He in the court of Egypt staid
Till he most falsely was betrayed.

(Condensed.) Old Ballad.

THE DAY-DREAM

The Sleeping Palace

I

THE varying year with blade and sheaf
  Clothes and reclothes the happy plains;
Here rests the sap within the leaf,
  Here stays the blood along the veins.
Faint shadows, vapors lightly curl'd,
  Faint murmurs from the meadows come,

Like hints and echoes of the world
　To spirits folded in the womb.

II

Soft luster bathes the range of urns
　On every slanting terrace-lawn.
The fountain to his place returns
　Deep in the garden lake withdrawn.
Here droops the banner on the tower,
　On the hall-hearths the festal fires,
The peacock in his laurel bower,
　The parrot in his gilded wires.

III

Roof-haunting martins warm their eggs:
　In these, in those the life is stay'd.
The mantles from the golden pegs
　Droop sleepily; no sound is made,
Not even of a gnat that sings.
　More like a picture seemeth all
Than those old portraits of old kings,
　That watch the sleepers from the wall.

IV

Here sits the butler with a flask
　Between his knees, half-drain'd; and there
The wrinkled steward at his task,
　The maid-of-honor blooming fair,

The page has caught her hand in his;
  Her lips are sever'd as to speak;
His own are pouted to a kiss:
  The blush is fix'd upon her cheek.

V

Till all the hundred summers pass,
  The beams, that thro' the Oriel shine,
Make prisms in every carven glass,
  And beaker brimm'd with noble wine.
Each baron at the banquet sleeps,
  Grave faces gather'd in a ring.
His state the King reposing keeps.
  He must have been a jovial king.

VI

All round a hedge upshoots, and shows
  At distance like a little wood;
Thorns, ivies, woodbine, mistletoes,
  And grapes with bunches red as blood;
All creeping plants, a wall of green
  Close-matted, burr and brake and brier,
And glimpsing over these, just seen,
  High up, the topmost palace-spire.

VII

When will the hundred summers die,
  And thought and time be born again,

And newer knowledge, drawing nigh,
  Bring truth that sways the soul of men?
Here all things in their place remain,
  As all were order'd, ages since.
Come, Care and Pleasure, Hope and Pain,
  And bring the fated fairy Prince.

The Sleeping Beauty

I

Year after year unto her feet,
  She lying on her couch alone,
Across the purple coverlet,
  The maiden's jet-black hair has grown,
On either side her tranced form
  Forth streaming from a braid of pearl;
The slumbrous light is rich and warm,
  And moves not on the rounded curl.

II

The silk star-broider'd coverlid
  Unto her limbs itself doth mould
Languidly ever; and, amid
  Her full black ringlets downward roll'd,
Glows forth each softly-shadow'd arm
  With bracelets of the diamond bright:
Her constant beauty doth inform
  Stillness with love, and day with light.

III

She sleeps; her breathings are not heard
  In palace chambers far apart.
The fragrant tresses are not stirr'd
  That lie upon her charmed heart.
She sleeps; on either hand upswells
  The gold-fringed pillow lightly prest;
She sleeps, nor dreams, but ever dwells
  A perfect form in perfect rest.

The Arrival

I

All precious things, discover'd late,
  To those that seek them issue forth;
For love in sequel works with fate,
  And draws the veil from hidden worth.
He travels far from other skies —
  His mantle glitters on the rocks —
A fairy Prince, with joyful eyes,
  And lighter-footed than the fox.

II

The bodies and the bones of those
  That strove in other days to pass,
Are wither'd in the thorny close,
  Or scatter'd blanching on the grass.
He gazes on the silent dead:
  "They perish'd in their daring deeds."

This proverb flashes thro' his head,
  "The many fail; the one succeeds."

III

He comes, scarce knowing what he seeks;
  He breaks the hedge; he enters there;
The color flies into his cheeks:
  He trusts to light on something fair;
For all his life the charm did talk
  About his path, and hover near
With words of promise in his walk,
  And whisper'd voices at his ear.

IV

More close and close his footsteps wind;
  The Magic Music in his heart,
Beats quick and quicker, till he find
  The quiet chamber far apart.
His spirit flutters like a lark,
  He stoops — to kiss her — on his knee.
"Love, if thy tresses be so dark,
  How dark those hidden eyes must be!"

The Revival

I

A touch, a kiss! the charm was snapt.
  There rose a noise of striking clocks,
And feet that ran, and doors that clapt,
  And barking dogs, and crowing cocks;

A fuller light illumined all,
  A breeze thro’ all the garden swept,
A sudden hubbub shook the hall,
  And sixty feet the fountain leapt.

II

The hedge broke in, the banner blew.
  The butler drank, the steward scrawl’d,
The fire shot up, the martin flew,
  The parrot scream’d, the peacock squall’d,
The maid and page renew’d their strife,
  The palace bang’d, and buzz’d and clackt,
And all the long-pent stream of life
  Dash’d downward in a cataract.

III

And last with these the King awoke,
  And in his chair himself uprear’d,
And yawn’d, and rubb’d his face, and spoke:
  “By holy rood, a royal beard!
How say you? we have slept, my lords.
  My beard has grown into my lap.”
The barons swore, with many words,
  ’T was but an after-dinner’s nap.

IV

“Pardy,” return’d the King, “but still
  My joints are somewhat stiff or so.

My lord, and shall we pass the bill
  I mention'd half an hour ago?"
The chancellor, sedate and vain,
  In courteous words return'd reply;
But dallied with his golden chain,
  And, smiling, put the question by.

The Departure

I

And on her lover's arm she leant,
  And round her waist she felt it fold,
And far across the hills they went
  In that new world which is the old;
Across the hills, and far away
  Beyond their utmost purple rim,
And deep into the dying day
  The happy Princess follow'd him.

II

"I'd sleep another hundred years,
  O love, for such another kiss;"
"O wake for ever, love," she hears,
  "O love, 't was such as this and this."
And o'er them many a sliding star,
  And many a merry wind was borne,
And, stream'd thro' many a golden bar,
  The twilight melted into morn.

III

"O eyes long laid in happy sleep!"
  "O happy sleep, that lightly fled!"
"O happy kiss, that woke thy sleep!"
  "O love, thy kiss would wake the dead!"
And o'er them many a flowing range
  Of vapor buoy'd the crescent-bark,
And, rapt thro' many a rosy change,
  The twilight died into the dark.

IV

"A hundred summers! can it be?
  And whither goest thou, tell me where?"
"O seek my father's court with me,
  For there are greater wonders there."
And o'er the hills, and far away
  Beyond their utmost purple rim,
Beyond the night, across the day,
  Thro' all the world she follow'd him.

Alfred Lord Tennyson.

JOLLY RHYMES AND POEMS

THE OWL AND THE PUSSY-CAT

The Owl and the Pussy-Cat went to sea
  In a beautiful pea-green boat;
They took some honey, and plenty of money
  Wrapped up in a five-pound note.
The Owl looked up to the moon above,
  And sang to a small guitar:
"O lovely Pussy! O Pussy, my love!
  What a beautiful Pussy you are, —
        You are,
  What a beautiful Pussy you are!"

Pussy said to the Owl: "You elegant fowl!
  How charmingly sweet you sing!
O let us be married, — too long we have
      tarried, —
  But what shall we do for a ring?"
They sailed away for a year and a day
  To the land where the Bong-tree grows,
And there in a wood, a piggy-wig stood
  With a ring in the end of his nose, —
        His nose,
  With a ring in the end of his nose.

"Dear Pig, are you willing to sell for one
      shilling
  Your ring?" Said the piggy, "I will."

So they took it away, and were married next
        day
By the turkey who lives on the hill.
They dined upon mince and slices of quince,
    Which they ate with a runcible spoon,
And hand in hand on the edge of the sand
    They danced by the light of the moon, —
            The moon,
    They danced by the light of the moon.

Edward Lear.

THE DONKEY AND THE
MOCKING-BIRD

A MOCK-BIRD in a village
    Had somehow gained the skill
To imitate the voices
    Of animals at will.

And, singing in his prison
    Once, at the close of day,
He gave, with great precision,
    The donkey's heavy bray.

Well pleased, the mock-bird's master
    Sent to the neighbors 'round,
And bade them come together
    To hear that curious sound.

They came, and all were talking
  In praise of what they heard,
And one delighted lady
  Would fain have bought the bird.

A donkey listened sadly,
  And said: "Confess I must
That these are stupid people,
  And terribly unjust.

"I'm bigger than the mock-bird,
  And better bray than he,
Yet not a soul has uttered
  A word in praise of me."

From the Spanish of José Rosas.
Translated by W. C. Bryant.

THE OLD MAN WHO LIVED
IN A WOOD

There was an old man who lived in a wood,
  As you may plainly see;
He said he could do as much work in a day,
  As his wife could do in three.
"With all my heart," the old woman said,
  "If that you will allow,
To-morrow you'll stay at home in my stead,
  And I'll go drive the plough;

"But you must milk the Tidy cow,
  For fear that she go dry;
And you must feed the little pigs
  That are within the sty;
And you must mind the speckled hen,
  For fear she lay away;
And you must reel the spool of yarn
  That I span yesterday."

The old woman took a staff in her
    hand,
  And went to drive the plough;
The old man took a pail in his hand,
  And went to milk the cow;
But Tidy hinched, and Tidy flinched,
  And Tidy broke his nose,
And Tidy gave him such a blow,
  That the blood ran down to his toes.

"High! Tidy! ho! Tidy! high!
  Tidy, do stand still!
If ever I milk you, Tidy, again,
  'T will be sore against my will."

He went to feed the little pigs,
  That were within the sty;
He hit his head against the beam
  And he made the blood to fly.

He went to mind the speckled hen,
  For fear she'd lay astray,
And he forgot the spool of yarn
  His wife spun yesterday.

So he swore by the sun, the moon, and the stars,
  And the green leaves on the tree,
If his wife did n't do a day's work in her life,
  She should ne'er be ruled by he.

Old Rhyme.

THE ENCHANTED SHIRT

*Fytte the First: wherein it shall be shown how the Truth
is too mighty a Drug for such as be of feeble temper.*

THE King was sick. His cheek was red,
  And his eye was clear and bright;
He ate and drank with kingly zest,
  And peacefully snored at night.

But he said he was sick, and a king should
      know,
  And the doctors came by the score.
They did not cure him. He cut off their heads,
  And sent to the schools for more.

At last two famous doctors came,
  And one was as poor as a rat, —

He had passed his life in studious toil,
  And never found time to grow fat.

The other had never looked in a book;
  His patients gave him no trouble:
If they recovered, they paid him well;
  If they died, their heirs paid double.

Together they looked at the royal tongue,
  As the King on his couch reclined;
In succession they thumped his august chest,
  But no trace of disease could find.

The old Sage said: "You're as sound as a
    nut."
"Hang him up," roared the King in a gale —
In a ten-knot gale of royal rage;
  The other leech grew a shade pale;

But he pensively rubbed his sagacious nose,
  And thus his prescription ran —
The King will be well, if he sleeps one night
  In the Shirt of a Happy Man.

*Fytte the Second: tells of the search for the Shirt and
how it was nigh found but was not, for reasons which
are said or sung.*

Wide o'er the realm the couriers rode,
  And fast their horses ran,

And many they saw, and to many they spoke,
    But they found no Happy Man.

They found poor men who would fain be
        rich,
    And rich who thought they were poor;
And men who twisted their waists in stays,
    And women who short hose wore.

At last they came to a village gate,
    A beggar lay whistling there;
He whistled, and sang, and laughed, and
        rolled
    On the grass, in the soft June air.

The weary couriers paused and looked
    At the scamp so blithe and gay;
And one of them said: "Heaven save you,
        friend!
    You seem to be happy to-day."

"O yes, fair sirs," the rascal laughed,
    And his voice rang free and glad;
"An idle man has so much to do
    That he never has time to be sad."

"This is our man," the courier said;
    "Our luck has led us aright.

I will give you a hundred ducats, friend,
  For the loan of your shirt to-night."

The merry blackguard lay back on the grass,
  And laughed till his face was black;
"I would do it, God wot," and he roared
    with the fun,
  "But I have n't a shirt to my back."

*Fytte the Third: shewing how His Majesty the King
came at last to sleep in a Happy Man his Shirt.*

Each day to the King the reports came in
  Of his unsuccessful spies,
And the sad panorama of human woes
  Passed daily under his eyes.

And he grew ashamed of his useless life,
  And his maladies hatched in gloom;
He opened his windows and let the air
  Of the free heaven into his room.

And out he went in the world, and toiled
  In his own appointed way;
And the people blessed him, the land was
    glad,
  And the King was well and gay.

John Hay.

THE DIVERTING HISTORY OF
JOHN GILPIN

*Showing How He Went Farther Than He Intended, and
Came Safe Home Again*

John Gilpin was a citizen
  Of credit and renown,
A train-band Captain eke was he
  Of famous London town.

John Gilpin's spouse said to her dear:
  "Though wedded we have been
These twice ten tedious years, yet we
  No holiday have seen.

"To-morrow is our wedding day,
  And we will then repair
Unto the Bell at Edmonton,
  All in a chaise and pair.

"My sister, and my sister's child,
  Myself and children three,
Will fill the chaise, so you must ride
  On horseback after we."

He soon replied: — "I do admire
  Of womankind but one,
And you are she, my dearest dear,
  Therefore it shall be done.

"I am a linen-draper bold,
  As all the world doth know,
And my good friend the Calender
  Will lend his horse to go."

Quoth Mrs. Gilpin: — "That's well said;
  And, for that wine is dear,
We will be furnish'd with our own,
  Which is both bright and clear."

John Gilpin kiss'd his loving wife;
  O'erjoyed was he to find,
That, though on pleasure she was bent,
  She had a frugal mind.

The morning came, the chaise was brought,
  But yet was not allow'd
To drive up to the door, lest all
  Should say that she was proud.

So three doors off the chaise was stay'd,
  Where they did all get in;
Six precious souls, and all agog
  To dash through thick and thin.

Smack went the whip, round went the wheels,
  Were never folk so glad;
The stones did rattle underneath,
  As if Cheapside were mad.

John Gilpin at his horse's side
  Seized fast the flowing mane,
And up he got, in haste to ride,
  But soon came down again;

For saddle-tree scarce reach'd had he,
  His journey to begin,
When, turning round his head, he saw
  Three customers come in.

So down he came; for loss of time,
  Although it grieved him sore,
Yet loss of pence, full well he knew,
  Would trouble him much more.

'T was long before the customers
  Were suited to their mind,
When Betty screaming, came downstairs:
  "The wine is left behind!"

"Good lack!" quoth he,—"yet bring it me,
  My leathern belt likewise,
In which I bear my trusty sword,
  When I do exercise."

Now Mistress Gilpin (careful soul!)
  Had two stone bottles found,
To hold the liquor that she loved,
  And keep it safe and sound.

Each bottle had a curling ear,
  Through which the belt he drew,
And hung a bottle on each side,
  To make his balance true.

Then over all, that he might be
  Equipp'd from top to toe,
His long red cloak, well brush'd and neat,
  He manfully did throw.

Now see him mounted once again
  Upon his nimble steed,
Full slowly pacing o'er the stones,
  With caution and good heed.

But finding soon a smoother road
  Beneath his well-shod feet,
The snorting beast began to trot,
  Which gall'd him in his seat,

So "Fair and softly," John he cried,
  But John he cried in vain;
That trot became a gallop soon,
  In spite of curb and rein.

So stooping down, as needs he must
  Who cannot sit upright,
He grasp'd the mane with both his hands,
  And eke with all his might.

His horse, who never in that sort
  Had handled been before,
What thing upon his back had got
  Did wonder more and more.

Away went Gilpin, neck or nought;
  Away went hat and wig;
He little dreamt, when he set out,
  Of running such a rig!

The wind did blow, the cloak did fly,
  Like streamer long and gay,
Till, loop and button failing both,
  At last it flew away.

Then might all people well discern
  The bottles he had slung;
A bottle swinging at each side,
  As hath been said or sung.

The dogs did bark, the children scream'd,
  Up flew the windows all,
And ev'ry soul cried out: "Well done!"
  As loud as he could bawl.

Away went Gilpin — who but he?
  His fame soon spread around;
"He carries weight!" "He rides a race!"
  "'T is for a thousand pound!"

And still, as fast as he drew near,
    'T was wonderful to view,
How in a trice the turnpike-men
    Their gates wide open threw.

And now, as he went bowing down
    His reeking head full low,
The bottles twain behind his back
    Were shattered at a blow.

Down ran the wine into the road,
    Most piteous to be seen,
Which made his horse's flanks to smoke
    As they had basted been.

But still he seem'd to carry weight,
    With leathern girdle braced,
For all might see the bottle-necks
    Still dangling at his waist.

Thus all through merry Islington
    These gambols he did play,
Until he came unto the Wash
    Of Edmonton so gay;

And there he threw the Wash about
    On both sides of the way,
Just like unto a trundling mop,
    Or a wild-goose at play.

At Edmonton his loving wife
  From the balcony spied
Her tender husband, wond'ring much
  To see how he did ride.

"Stop, stop, John Gilpin! — Here's the
     house!"
  They all at once did cry;
"The dinner waits and we are tired:"
  Said Gilpin: "So am I!"

But yet his horse was not a whit
  Inclined to tarry there;
For why? — his owner had a house
  Full ten miles off, at Ware.

So like an arrow swift he flew,
  Shot by an archer strong;
So did he fly — which brings me to
  The middle of my song.

Away went Gilpin, out of breath,
  And sore against his will,
Till at his friend the Calender's
  His horse at last stood still.

The Calender, amazed to see
  His neighbour in such trim,
Laid down his pipe, flew to the gate,
  And thus accosted him: —

"What news? what news? your tidings tell,
  Tell me you must and shall —
Say why bare-headed you are come,
  Or why you come at all?"

Now Gilpin had a pleasant wit,
  And loved a timely joke,
And thus unto the Calender
  In merry guise he spoke: —

"I came because your horse would come;
  And, if I well forebode,
My hat and wig will soon be here,
  They are upon the road."

The Calender, right glad to find
  His friend in merry pin,
Return'd him not a single word,
  But to the house went in;

Whence straight he came with hat and wig;
  A wig that flow'd behind,
A hat not much the worse for wear,
  Each comely in its kind.

He held them up, and in his turn
  Thus show'd his ready wit: —
"My head is twice as big as yours,
  They therefore needs must fit.

"But let me scrape the dirt away
  That hangs upon your face;
And stop and eat, for well you may
  Be in a hungry case."

Said John: — "It is my wedding day,
  And all the world would stare,
If wife should dine at Edmonton,
  And I should dine at Ware."

So, turning to his horse, he said:
  "I am in haste to dine;
'T was for your pleasure you came here,
  You shall go back for mine."

Ah, luckless speech, and bootless boast!
  For which he paid full dear;
For, while he spake, a braying ass
  Did sing most loud and clear;

Whereat his horse did snort, as he
  Had heard a lion roar,
And gallop'd off with all his might,
  As he had done before.

Away went Gilpin, and away
  Went Gilpin's hat and wig;
He lost them sooner than at first,
  For why? — they were too big!

Now Mistress Gilpin, when she saw
  Her husband posting down
Into the country far away,
  She pull'd out half-a-crown;

And thus unto the youth she said
  That drove them to the Bell:
"This shall be yours when you bring back
  My husband safe and well."

The youth did ride, and soon did meet
  John coming back amain;
Whom in a trice he tried to stop,
  By catching at his rein;

But not performing what he meant,
  And gladly would have done,
The frighted steed he frighted more,
  And made him faster run.

Away went Gilpin, and away
  Went post-boy at his heels! —
The post-boy's horse right glad to miss
  The lumb'ring of the wheels.

Six gentlemen upon the road,
  Thus seeing Gilpin fly,
With post-boy scamp'ring in the rear,
  They raised the hue and cry: —

"Stop thief! stop thief — a highwayman!"
  Not one of them was mute;
And all and each that pass'd that way
  Did join in the pursuit.

And now the turnpike gates again
  Flew open in short space;
The toll-men thinking, as before,
  That Gilpin rode a race.

And so he did, and won it too,
  For he got first to town,
Nor stopp'd till where he had got up
  He did again get down.

Now let us sing, Long live the King!
  And Gilpin, long live he!
And, when he next doth ride abroad,
  May I be there to see!

William Cowper.

THE WHITE STAG

INTO the woods three huntsmen came,
Seeking the white stag for their game.

They laid them under a green fir-tree
And slept, and dreamed strange things to see.

(*First huntsman*)

"I dreamt I was beating the leafy brush,
When out popped the noble stag — hush,
     hush!"

(*Second huntsman*)

"As ahead of the clamorous pack he sprang,
I pelted him hard in the hide — piff, bang!"

(*Third huntsman*)

"And as that stag lay dead I blew
On my horn a lusty tir-ril-la-loo!"

So speak, the three as there they lay,
When lo! the white stag sped that way,
Frisked his heels at those huntsmen three,
Then leagues o'er hill and dale was he —
Hush, hush! Piff, bang! Tir-ril-la-loo!

From the German of Ludwig Uhland.
Translated by Eugene Field.

THE YARN OF THE NANCY BELL

'T was on the shores that round our coast
   From Deal to Ramsgate span,
That I found alone on a piece of stone
   An elderly naval man.

His hair was weedy, his beard was long,
 And weedy and long was he,
And I heard this wight on the shore recite,
 In a singular minor key:

"Oh, I am a cook and a captain bold,
 And the mate of the Nancy brig,
And a bo'sun tight, and the midshipmite,
 And the crew of the captain's gig."

And he shook his fists and he tore his hair,
 Till I really felt afraid,
For I could n't help thinking the man had
  been drinking,
 And so I simply said:

"Oh, elderly man, it's little I know
 Of the duties of men of the sea,
And I'll eat my hand if I understand
 However you can be

"At once a cook, and a captain bold,
 And the mate of the Nancy brig,
And a bo'sun tight, and a midshipmite,
 And the crew of the captain's gig."

Then he gave a hitch to his trousers, which
 Is a trick all seamen larn,
And having got rid of a thumping quid,
 He spun this painful yarn:

"'T was in the good ship Nancy Bell
  That we sailed to the Indian Sea,
And there on a reef we came to grief,
  Which has often occurred to me.

"And pretty nigh all the crew was drowned
  (There was seventy-seven o' soul),
And only ten of the Nancy's men
  Said 'Here!' to the muster-roll.

"There was me and the cook and the captain
    bold,
  And the mate of the Nancy brig,
And a bo'sun tight, and a midshipmite,
  And the crew of the captain's gig.

"For a month we'd neither wittles nor drink,
  Till a-hungry we did feel.
So we draw'd a lot, and, accordin' shot
  The captain for our meal.

"The next lot fell to the Nancy's mate
  And a delicate dish he made;
Then our appetite with the midshipmite
  We seven survivors stayed.

"And then we murdered the bo'sun tight,
  And he much resembled pig;
Then we wittled free, did the cook and me,
  On the crew of the captain's gig.

"Then only the cook and me was left,
　And the delicate question, 'Which
Of us goes to the kettle?' arose
　And we argued it out as sich.

"For I loved that cook as a brother, I did,
　And the cook he worshipped me;
But we'd both be blowed if we'd either be
　　stowed
　In the other chap's hold, you see.

"'I'll be eat if you dines off me,' says Tom;
　'Yes, that,' says I, 'you'll be —
I'm boiled if I die, my friend,' quoth I;
　And 'Exactly so,' quoth he.

"Says he: 'Dear James, to murder me
　Were a foolish thing to do,
For don't you see that you can't cook *me*,
　While I can — and will — cook *you!*'

"So he boils the water, and takes the salt
　And the pepper in portions true
(Which he never forgot), and some chopped
　　shalot,
　And some sage and parsley too.

"'Come here,' says he, with a proper pride
　Which his smiling features tell,
''T will soothing be if I let you see
　How extremely nice you'll smell.'

"And he stirred it round and round and round,
  And he sniffed at the foaming froth;
When I ups with his heels, and smothers his
    squeals
In the scum of the boiling broth.

"And I eat that cook in a week or less,
  And — as I eating be
The last of his chops, why, I almost drops,
  For a wessel in sight I see!

  .   .   .   .

"And I never larf, and I never smile,
  And I never lark nor play,
But sit and croak, and a single joke
  I have — which is to say:

"Oh, I am a cook and a captain bold,
  And the mate of the Nancy brig.
And a bo'sun tight, and a midshipmite,
  And the crew of the captain's gig!"

                        W. S. Gilbert.

FAITHLESS NELLY GRAY

BEN BATTLE was a soldier bold,
  And used to war's alarms;
But a cannon ball took off his legs,
  So he laid down his arms!

Now as they bore him off the field,
  Said he: "Let others shoot,
For here I leave my second leg,
  And the Forty-Second Foot!"

The army-surgeons made him limbs:
  Said he:—"They're only pegs;
But there's as wooden members quite
  As represent my legs!"

Now Ben he loved a pretty maid,
  Her name was Nelly Gray;
So he went to pay her his devours
  When he'd devoured his pay!

But when he called on Nelly Gray,
  She made him quite a scoff;
And when she saw his wooden legs,
  Began to take them off!

"O Nelly Gray! O Nelly Gray!
  Is this your love so warm?
The love that loves a scarlet coat
  Should be more uniform!"

She said: "I loved a soldier once,
  For he was blithe and brave;
But I will never have a man
  With both legs in the grave!

"Before you had those timber toes,
    Your love I did allow,
But then, you know, you stand upon
    Another footing now!"

"O Nelly Gray! O Nelly Gray!
    For all your jeering speeches,
At duty's call I left my legs
    In Badajos's *breaches !*"

"Why then," said she, "you've lost the feet
    Of legs in war's alarms,
And now you cannot wear your shoes
    Upon your feats of arms!"

"Oh, false and fickle Nelly Gray,
    I know why you refuse: —
Though I've no feet — some other man
    Is standing in my shoes!

"I wish I ne'er had seen your face;
    But now a long farewell!
For you will be my death; — alas!
    You will not be my *Nell !*"

Now when he went from Nelly Gray,
    His heart so heavy got —
And life was such a burthen grown,
    It made him take a knot!

So round his melancholy neck
  A rope he did entwine,
And, for his second time in life,
  Enlisted in the Line!

One end he tied around a beam
  And then removed his pegs,
And, as his legs were off, — of course
  He soon was off his legs!

And there he hung till he was dead
  As any nail in town, —
For though distress had cut him up,
  It could not cut him down!

A dozen men sat on his corpse,
  To find out why he died —
And they buried Ben in four cross-roads,
  With a *stake* in his inside!

Thomas Hood.

THE KING AND THE MILLER OF MANSFIELD

HENRY, our royal king, would ride a-hunting
  To the green forest so pleasant and fair;
To see the harts skipping, and dainty does
    tripping,

Unto merry Sherwood his nobles repair:
Hawk and hound were unbound, all things
          prepar'd
For the game, in the same, with good regard.

All a long summer's day rode the king pleas-
          antly,
    With all his princes and nobles each one;
Chasing the hart and hind, and the buck gal-
          lantly,
    Till the dark evening forced all to turn home.
Then at last, riding fast, he had lost quite
All his lords in the wood, late in the night.

Wandering thus wearily, all alone, up and
          down,
    With a rude miller he met at the last;
Asking the ready way unto fair Nottingham,
    "Sir," quoth the miller, "I mean not to
          jest,
Yet I think, what I think, sooth for to say;
You do not lightly ride out of your way."

"Why, what dost thou think of me," quoth
          our king merrily,
    "Passing thy judgment upon me so brief?"
"Good faith," said the miller, "I mean not
          to flatter thee,
    I guess thee to be but some gentleman
          thief;

Stand thee back, in the dark; light not
  adown,
Lest that I presently crack thy knave's
  crown."

"Thou dost abuse me much," quoth the king,
    "saying thus;
  I am a gentleman; lodging I lack."
"Thou hast not," quoth th' miller, "one groat
    in thy purse;
  All thy inheritance hangs on thy back."
"I have gold to discharge all that I call;
If it be forty pence, I will pay all."

"If thou beest a true man," then quoth the
    miller,
  "I swear by my toll-dish, I'll lodge thee all
    night."
"Here's my hand," quoth the king, "that
    was I ever."
  "Nay, soft," quoth the miller, "thou may'st
    be a sprite.
Better I'll know thee, ere hands we will shake;
With none but honest men hands will I take."

Thus they went all along unto the miller's
    house,
  Where they were seething of puddings and
    souse;

The miller first enter'd in, after him went the
    king;
  Never came he in soe smoky a house.
"Now," quoth he, "let me see here what you
    are."
Quoth our king, "Look your fill, and do not
    spare."

"I like well thy countenance, thou hast an
    honest face:
  With my son Richard this night thou shalt
    lie."
Quoth his wife, "By my troth, it is a hand-
    some youth,
  Yet it's best, husband, to deal warily.
Art thou no run-away, prythee, youth, tell?
Show me thy passport, and all shall be well."

Then our king presently, making low cour-
    tesy,
  With his hat in his hand, thus he did say;
"I have no passport, nor never was servitor,
  But a poor courtier rode out of my way:
And for your kindness here offered to me,
I will requite you in every degree."

Then to the miller his wife whisper'd secretly,
  Saying: "It seemeth, this youth's of good
    kin,

Both by his apparel, and eke by his manners;
  To turn him out, certainly were a great
       sin."
"Yea," quoth he, "you may see he hath some
      grace,
When he doth speak to his betters in place."

"Well," quo' the miller's wife, "young man,
      ye 're welcome here;
  And, though I say it, well lodged shall
      be:
Fresh straw will I have, laid on thy bed so
      brave,
  And good brown hempen sheets likewise,"
      quoth she.
"Aye," quoth the good man; "and when
      that is done,
Thou shalt lie with no worse than our own
      son."

This caused the king, suddenly, to laugh most
      heartily,
  Till the tears trickled fast down from his
      eyes.
Then to their supper were they set orderly,
  With hot bag-puddings, and good apple-
      pies;
Nappy ale, good and stale, in a brown bowl,
Which did about the board merrily troll.

"Here," quoth the miller, "good fellow, I
        drink to thee."
"I pledge thee," quoth our king, "and
        thank thee heartily
For my good welcome in every degree:
And here, in like manner, I drink to thy son."
"Do then," quoth Richard, "and quicke let
        it come."

"Wife," quoth the miller, "fetch me forth
        lightfoot,
    And of his sweetness a little we'll taste."
A fair ven'son pasty brought she out pres-
            ently,
    "Eat," quoth the miller, "but, sir, make no
        waste.
Here's dainty lightfoot!" "In faith," said the
        king,
"I never before eat so dainty a thing."

"I wis," quoth Richard, "no dainty at all
        it is,
    For we do eate of it every day."
"In what place," said our king, "may be
        bought like to this?"
"We never pay penny for it, by my fay:
From merry Sherwood we fetch it home here;
Now and then we make bold with our king's
        deer."

"Then I think," said our king, "that it is
        venison."
    "Each fool," quoth Richard, "full well
        may know that:
Never are we without two or three in the roof,
    Very well fleshed, and excellent fat:
But, prythee, say nothing wherever thou go;
We would not, for twopence, the king should
        it know."

"Doubt not," then said the king, "my prom-
        ised secresy;
    The king shall never know more on't for
        me."
A cup of lamb's-wool[1] they drank unto him
        then,
    And to their beds they past presently.
The nobles, next morning, went all up and
        down,
    For to seek out the king in every town.

At last at the miller's "cot" soone they espied
        him out,
    As he was mounting upon his fair steed;
To whom they came presently, falling down
        on their knee;
    Which made the miller's heart wofully bleed;

[1] Ale and roasted apples.

Shaking and quaking, before him he stood,
Thinking he should have been hanged, by the
    rood.

The king, perceiving him fearfully trembling,
    Drew forth his sword, but nothing he said;
The miller down did fall, crying before them
    all,
    Doubting the king would have cut off his
    head.
But he his kind courtesy for to requite,
Gave him great living, and dubbed him a
    knight.

(Condensed.) Old Ballad.

KING JOHN AND THE ABBOT OF CANTERBURY

AN ancient story I'll tell you anon
Of a notable prince, that was called King
    John;
And he ruled England with main and with
    might,
For he did great wrong, and maintained little
    right.

And I'll tell you a story, a story so merry,
Concerning the Abbot of Canterbury;

How for his housekeeping, and high renown,
They rode post for him to fair London town.

An hundred men, the King did hear say,
The Abbot kept in his house every day;
And fifty gold chains, without any doubt,
In velvet coats waited the Abbot about.

"How now, Father Abbot, I hear it of thee,
Thou keepest a far better house than me;
And for thy housekeeping and high renown,
I fear thou work'st treason against my
     crown."

"My liege," quo' the Abbot, "I would it were
     knowne,
I never spend nothing but what is my owne;
And I trust your Grace will do me no deere,[1]
For spending of my owne true-gotten gear."

"Yes, yes, Father Abbot, thy fault it is highe,
And now for the same thou needest must dye;
For except thou canst answer me questions
     three,
Thy head shall be smitten from thy bodie.

"And first," quo' the King, "when I'm in
     this stead,
With my crowne of golde so faire on my head,

---

[1] Deere = hurt, mischief.

Among all my liege-men so noble of birthe,
Thou must tell to one penny what I am
    worthe.

"Secondlye, tell me, without any doubt,
How soone I may ride the whole world
    about,
And at the third question thou must not
    shrink,
But tell me here truly what I do think."

"Oh, these are hard questions for my shallow
    witt,
Nor I cannot answer your Grace as yet;
But if you will give me but three weekes
    space,
I'll do my endeavour to answer your Grace."

"Now three weeks' space to thee will I give,
And that is the longest time thou hast to
    live;
For if thou dost not answer my questions
    three,
Thy lands and thy livings are forfeit to me."

Away rode the Abbot all sad at that word,
And he rode to Cambridge, and Oxenford;
But never a doctor there was so wise,
That could with his learning an answer devise.

Then home rode the Abbot of comfort so cold,
And he met his Shepherd a-going to fold:
"How now, my Lord Abbot, you are welcome
   home;
What news do you bring us from good King
   John?"

"Sad news, sad news, Shepherd, I must give,
That I have but three days more to live;
For if I do not answer him questions three,
My head will be smitten from my bodie.

"The first is to tell him, there in that stead,
With his crown of gold so fair on his head,
Among all his liege men so noble of birth,
To within one penny of all what he is worth.

"The seconde, to tell him, without any doubt,
How soone he may ride this whole world
   about:
And at the third question I must not shrinke,
But tell him there truly what he does thinke."

"Now cheare up, Sire Abbot, did you never
   hear yet,
That a fool he may learne a wise man witt?
Lend me horse, and serving men, and your
   apparel,
And I'll ride to London to answere your
   quarrel.

"Nay frowne not, if it hath bin told unto
    mee,
I am like your Lordship, as ever may bee:
And if you will but lend me your gowne,
There is none shall knowe us at fair London
    towne."

"Now horses, and serving men thou shalt
    have,
With sumptuous array most gallant and
    brave;
With crozier, and mitre, and rochet, and cope,
Fit to appear 'fore our Father the Pope."

"Now welcome, Sire Abbot," the king he did
    say,
"'T is well thou 'rt come back to keepe thy
    day;
For and if thou canst answer my questions
    three,
Thy life and thy living both saved shall bee.

"And first, when thou seest me, here in this
    stead,
With my crown of golde so fair on my head,
Among all my liege men so noble of birthe,
Tell me to one penny what I am worth."

"For thirty pence our Saviour was sold
Among the false Jewes, as I have bin told:

And twenty-nine is the worth of thee,
For I thinke, thou art one penny worser than
      he."

The King he laughed, and swore by St. Bittel,
"I did not think I had been worth so little!
Now secondly tell me, without any doubt,
How soon I may ride this whole world about."

"You must rise with the sun, and ride with
      the same,
Until the next morning he riseth again;
And then your Grace need not make any
      doubt,
But in twenty-four hours you'll ride it about."

The King he laughed, and swore by St. Jone,
"I did not think it could be gone so soon.
Now from the third question thou must not
      shrink,
But tell me here truly what do I think."

"Yea, that I shall do, and make your Grace
      merry;
You think I'm the Abbot of Canterbury;
But I'm his poor shepherd, as plain you may
      see,
That am come to beg pardon for him and for
      me."

The King he laughed, and swore by the mass,
"I'll make thee Lord Abbot this day in his
    place!"
"Now, nay, my Liege, be not in such speed,
For alack, I can neither write nor read."

"Four nobles a week, then, I will give thee,
For this merry jest thou hast shown unto me;
And tell the old Abbot, when thou comest
    home,
Thou hast brought him a pardon from good
    King John."
      From Percy's Reliques of Ancient English Poetry.

THE WELL OF ST. KEYNE

A WELL there is in the west country,
  And a clearer one never was seen;
There is not a wife in the west country
  But has heard of the Well of St. Keyne.

An oak and an elm tree stand beside,
  And behind doth an ash tree grow,
And a willow from the bank above
  Droops to the water below.

A traveller came to the Well of St. Keyne;
  Joyfully he drew nigh,

For from cock-crow he had been travelling,
 And there was not a cloud in the sky.

He drank of the water so cool and clear,
 For thirsty and hot was he,
And he sat down upon the bank
 Under the willow tree.

There came a man from the house hard by
 At the Well to fill his pail;
On the Well-side he rested it,
 And he bade the Stranger hail.

"Now art thou a bachelor, Stranger?" quoth
    he,
 "For an' if thou hast a wife,
The happiest draught thou hast drank this day
 That ever thou didst in thy life.

"Or has thy good woman, if one thou hast,
 Ever here in Cornwall been?
For an' if she have, I'll venture my life
 She has drank of the Well of St. Keyne."

"I have left a good woman who never was
    here,"
 The Stranger he made reply,
"But that my draught should be the better
    for that,
 I pray you answer me why?"

"St. Keyne," quoth the Cornish-man, "many
    a time
  Drank of this crystal Well,
And before the Angel summon'd her,
  She laid on the water a spell.

"If the Husband of this gifted Well
  Shall drink before his Wife,
A happy man thenceforth is he,
  For he shall be Master for life.

"But if the Wife should drink of it first,
  God help the Husband then!"
The Stranger stoopt to the Well of St. Keyne,
  And drank of the water again.

"You drank of the Well I warrant betimes?"
  He to the Cornish-man said:
But the Cornish-man smiled as the Stranger
    spake,
  And sheepishly shook his head.

"I hasten'd as soon as the wedding was done,
  And left my Wife in the porch;
But i' faith she had been wiser than me,
  For she took a bottle to Church."

Robert Southey.

SAD POEMS

THE BABES IN THE WOOD

Now ponder well, you parents dear,
  These words which I shall write;
A doleful story you shall hear,
  In time brought forth to light.
A gentleman of good account
  In Norfolk dwelt of late,
Who did in honour far surmount
  Most men of his estate.

Sore sick he was, and like to die,
  No help his life could save;
His wife by him as sick did lie,
  And both possessed one grave.
No love between these two was lost,
  Each was to other kind;
In love they lived, in love they died,
  And left two babes behind.

The one a fine and pretty boy,
  Not passing three years old;
The other a girl more young than he,
  And framed in beauty's mould.
The father left his little son,
  As plainly doth appear,

When he to perfect age should come,
    Three hundred pounds a year.

And to his little daughter Jane
    Five hundred pounds in gold,
To be paid down on marriage-day,
    Which might not be controlled:
But if the children chance to die,
    Ere they to age should come,
Their uncle should possess their wealth;
    For so the will did run.

"Now, brother," said the dying man,
    "Look to my children dear;
Be good unto my boy and girl,
    No friends else have they here:
To God and you I recommend
    My children dear this day;
But little while be sure we have
    Within this world to stay.

"You must be father and mother both,
    And uncle all in one;
God knows what will become of them
    When I am dead and gone."
With that bespake their mother dear,
    "O brother kind," quoth she,
"You are the man must bring our babes
    To wealth or misery:

"And if you keep them carefully,
  Then God will you reward;
But if you otherwise should deal,
  God will your deeds regard."
With lips as cold as any stone,
  They kissed their children small:
"God bless you both, my children dear!"
  With that the tears did fall.

These speeches then their brother spoke
  To this sick couple there:
"The keeping of your little ones,
  Sweet sister, do not fear:
God never prosper me nor mine,
  Nor aught else that I have,
If I do wrong your children dear,
  When you are laid in grave."

The parents being dead and gone,
  The children home he takes,
And brings them straight unto his house,
  Where much of them he makes.
He had not kept these pretty babes
  A twelvemonth and a day,
But, for their wealth, he did devise
  To make them both away.

He bargained with two ruffians strong,
  Which were of furious mood,

That they should take these children young,
   And slay them in a wood.
He told his wife an artful tale,
   He would the children send,
To be brought up in fair London,
   With one that was his friend.

Away then went those pretty babes,
   Rejoicing at that tide,
Rejoicing with a merry mind,
   They should on cock-horse ride.
They prate and prattle pleasantly,
   As they rode on the way,
To those that should their butchers be,
   And work their lives' decay.

So that the pretty speech they had,
   Made Murder's heart relent;
And they that undertook the deed,
   Full sore did now repent.
Yet one of them more hard of heart,
   Did vow to do his charge,
Because the wretch, that hired him,
   Had paid him very large.

The other won't agree thereto,
   So here they fall to strife;
With one another they did fight
   About the children's life;

And he that was of mildest mood,
  Did slay the other there,
Within an unfrequented wood;
  The babes did quake for fear!

He took the children by the hand,
  Tears standing in their eye,
And bade them straightway follow him,
  And look they did not cry.
And two long miles he led them on,
  While they for food complain;
"Stay here," quoth he, "I'll bring you bread,
  When I come back again."

These pretty babes, with hand in hand,
  Went wandering up and down;
But never more could see the man
  Approaching from the town:
Their pretty lips with blackberries,
  Were all besmeared and dyed,
And when they saw the darksome night,
  They sat them down and cried.

Thus wandered these poor innocents,
  Till death did end their grief;
In one another's arms they died,
  As wanting due relief:
No burial this pretty pair
  Of any man receives,

Till Robin Redbreast piously
  Did cover them with leaves.

And now the heavy wrath of God
  Upon their uncle fell;
Yea, fearful fiends did haunt his house,
  His conscience felt an hell:
His barns were fired, his goods consumed,
  His lands were barren made,
His cattle died within the field,
  And nothing with him stayed.

And in a voyage to Portugal
  Two of his sons did die;
And to conclude, himself was brought
  To want and misery:
He pawned and mortgaged all his land
  Ere seven years came about;
And now at length this wicked act
  Did by this means come out:

The fellow that did take in hand
  These children for to kill,
Was for a robbery judged to die,
  Such was God's blessed will;
So did confess the very truth,
  As here hath been displayed;
Their uncle having died in gaol,
  Where he for debt was laid.

You that executors be made,
  And overseers eke
Of children that be fatherless,
  And infants mild and meek;
Take you example by this thing,
  And yield to each his right,
Lest God with such like misery
  Your wicked minds requite.

From Percy's Reliques of Ancient English Poetry.

THE PARROT

A PARROT, from the Spanish Main,
  Full young, and early caged, came o'er,
With bright wings, to the bleak domain
  Of Mulla's shore.

To spicy groves where he had won
  His plumage of resplendent hue,
His native fruits, and skies, and sun,
  He bade adieu.

For these he changed the smoke of turf,
  A heathery land and misty sky,
And turned on rocks and raging surf
  His golden eye.

But, petted, in our climate cold
  He lived and chattered many a day:

Until with age, from green and gold
  His wings grew gray.

At last, when blind and seeming dumb,
  He scolded, laugh'd, and spoke no more,
A Spanish stranger chanced to come
  To Mulla's shore.

He hailed the bird in Spanish speech,
  The bird in Spanish speech replied;
Flapped round his cage with joyous screech,
  Dropt down, and died.

Thomas Campbell.

BETH–GÊLERT; OR, THE GRAVE OF THE GREYHOUND

THE spearmen heard the bugle sound,
  And cheerily smiled the morn,
And many a brach and many a hound
  Obeyed Llewelyn's horn.

And still he blew a louder blast,
  And gave a lustier cheer:
"Come, Gêlert, come; wert never last
  Llewelyn's horn to hear.

"Oh! where does faithful Gêlert roam,
  The flower of all his race?

So true, so brave; a lamb at home,
    A lion in the chase!"

'T was only at Llewelyn's board
    The faithful Gêlert fed;
He watched, he served, he cheered his lord
    And sentinelled his bed.

In sooth, he was a peerless hound,
    The gift of royal John;
But now no Gêlert could be found,
    And all the chase rode on.

And now, as o'er the rocks and dells
    The gallant chidings rise,
All Snowdon's craggy chaos yells
    The many-mingled cries!

That day Llewelyn little loved
    The chase of hart or hare,
And scant and small the booty proved
    For Gêlert was not there.

Unpleased, Llewelyn homeward hied:
    When near the portal seat,
His truant Gêlert he espied
    Bounding his lord to greet.

But when he gained his castle-door,
    Aghast the chieftain stood:

The hound all o'er was smeared with gore,
   His lips, his fangs, ran blood.

Llewelyn gazed with fierce surprise:
   Unused such looks to meet,
His favorite checked his joyful guise,
   And crouched and licked his feet.

Onward in haste Llewelyn passed,
   And on went Gêlert too,
And still, where'er his eyes he cast,
   Fresh blood-gouts shocked his view.

O'erturned his infant's bed he found,
   With blood-stained covert rent,
And all around the walls and ground
   With recent blood besprent.

He called his child, no voice replied;
   He searched with terror wild;
Blood, blood, he found on every side;
   But nowhere found his child.

"Hell-hound! by thee my child's devoured!"
   The frantic father cried;
And to the hilt his vengeful sword
   He plunged in Gêlert's side.

His suppliant looks as prone he fell
   No pity could impart,

But still his Gêlert's dying yell
  Passed heavy o'er his heart.

Aroused by Gêlert's dying yell,
  Some slumberer wakened nigh:
What words the parent's joy could tell
  To hear his infant's cry!

Concealed beneath a tumbled heap
  His hurried search had missed,
All glowing from his rosy sleep,
  The cherub boy he kissed.

Nor scath had he, nor harm, nor dread;
  But the same couch beneath
Lay a gaunt wolf, all torn and dead,
  Tremendous still in death.

Ah, what was then Llewelyn's pain!
  For now the truth was clear;
The gallant hound the wolf had slain,
  To save Llewelyn's heir.

Vain, vain was all Llewelyn's woe:
  "Best of thy kind, adieu!
The frantic blow which laid thee low
  This heart shall ever rue."

And now a gallant tomb they raise,
  With costly sculpture deckt;

And marbles, storied with his praise,
  Poor Gêlert's bones protect.

There never could the spearman pass,
  Or forester, unmoved;
There oft the tear-besprinkled grass
  Llewelyn's sorrow proved.

And there he hung his sword and spear,
  And there, as evening fell,
In Fancy's ear he oft would hear
  Poor Gêlert's dying yell.

And till great Snowdon's rocks grow old,
  And cease the storm to brave,
The consecrated spot shall hold
  The name of "Gêlert's Grave."

William Robert Spencer.

THE CAPTAIN'S DAUGHTER

WE were crowded in the cabin,
  Not a soul would dare to sleep, —
It was midnight on the waters,
  And a storm was on the deep.

'T is a fearful thing in winter
  To be shattered by the blast,
And to hear the rattling trumpet
  Thunder, "Cut away the mast!"

So we shuddered there in silence, —
  For the stoutest held his breath,
While the hungry sea was roaring,
  And the breakers talked with Death.

As thus we sat in darkness,
  Each one busy with his prayers,
"We are lost!" the captain shouted,
  As he staggered down the stairs.

But his little daughter whispered,
  As she took his icy hand:
"Is n't God upon the ocean,
  Just the same as on the land?"

Then we kissed the little maiden,
  And we spoke in better cheer,
And we anchored safe in harbor
  When the morn was shining clear.
                    James Thomas Fields.

ALEC YEATON'S SON

Gloucester, August, 1720.

THE wind it wailed, the wind it moaned,
  And the white caps flecked the sea;
"An' I would to God," the skipper groaned,
  "I had not my boy with me!"

Snug in the stern-sheets, little John
  Laughed as the scud swept by;
But the skipper's sunburnt cheek grew wan
  As he watched the wicked sky.

"Would he were at his mother's side!"
  And the skipper's eyes were dim.
"Good Lord in heaven, if ill betide,
  What would become of him!

"For me, my muscles are as steel,
  For me let hap what may;
I might make shift upon the keel
  Until the break o' day.

"But he, he is so weak and small,
  So young, scarce learned to stand, —
O pitying Father of us all,
  I trust him in Thy hand!

"For Thou, who markest from on high
  A sparrow's fall, — each one! —
Surely, O Lord, Thou'lt have an eye
  On Alec Yeaton's son!"

Then, steady helm! Right straight he sailed
  Towards the headland light:
The wind it moaned, the wind it wailed,
  And black, black fell the night.

Then burst a storm to make one quail
  Though housed from winds and waves, —
They who could tell about that gale
  Must rise from watery graves!

Sudden it came, as sudden went;
  Ere half the night was sped,
The winds were hushed, the waves were
      spent,
  And the stars shone overhead.

Now, as the morning mist grew thin,
  The folk on Gloucester shore
Saw a little figure floating in,
  Secure, on a broken oar!

Up rose the cry: "A wreck! a wreck!
  Pull, mates, and waste no breath!"
They knew it, though 't was but a speck
  Upon the edge of death!

Long did they marvel in the town
  At God His strange decree,
That let the stalwart skipper drown,
  And the little child go free!

                    Thomas Bailey Aldrich.

THE WRECK OF THE HESPERUS

IT was the schooner Hesperus,
  That sailed the wintry sea;
And the skipper had taken his little daughtèr,
  To bear him company.

Blue were her eyes as the fairy-flax,
  Her cheeks like the dawn of day,
And her bosom white as the hawthorn buds,
  That ope in the month of May.

The skipper he stood beside the helm,
  His pipe was in his mouth,
And he watched how the veering flaw did blow
  The smoke now West, now South.

Then up and spake an old Sailòr,
  Had sailed to the Spanish Main,
"I pray thee, put into yonder port,
  For I fear a hurricane.

"Last night, the moon had a golden ring,
  And to-night no moon we see!"
The skipper, he blew a whiff from his pipe,
  And a scornful laugh laughed he.

Colder and louder blew the wind,
  A gale from the Northeast;

HE WRAPPED HER WARM IN HIS SEAMAN'S COAT

The snow fell hissing in the brine,
  And the billows frothed like yeast.

Down came the storm, and smote amain
  The vessel in its strength;
She shuddered and paused, like a frighted
      steed,
  Then leaped her cable's length.

"Come hither! come hither! my little
      daughtèr,
  And do not tremble so;
For I can weather the roughest gale
  That ever wind did blow."

He wrapped her warm in his seaman's coat
  Against the stinging blast;
He cut a rope from a broken spar,
  And bound her to the mast.

"O father! I hear the church-bells ring,
  O say, what may it be?"
"'T is a fog-bell on a rock-bound coast!"
  And he steered for the open sea.

"O father! I hear the sound of guns,
  O say, what may it be?"
"Some ship in distress, that cannot live
  In such an angry sea!"

"O father! I see a gleaming light,
  O say, what may it be?"
But the father answered never a word,
  A frozen corpse was he.

Lashed to the helm, all stiff and stark,
  With his face turned to the skies,
The lantern gleamed through the gleaming
      snow
  On his fixed and glassy eyes.

Then the maiden clasped her hands and
      prayed
  That savèd she might be;
And she thought of Christ, who stilled the
      wave
  On the Lake of Galilee.

And fast through the midnight dark and
      drear,
  Through the whistling sleet and snow,
Like a sheeted ghost the vessel swept
  Tow'rds the reef of Norman's Woe.

And ever the fitful gusts between
  A sound came from the land;
It was the sound of the trampling surf
  On the rocks and the hard sea-sand.

The breakers were right beneath her bows,
  She drifted a dreary wreck,
And a whooping billow swept the crew
  Like icicles from her deck.

She struck where the white and fleecy waves
  Looked soft as carded wool,
But the cruel rocks, they gored her side
  Like the horns of an angry bull.

Her rattling shrouds, all sheathed in ice,
  With the masts went by the board;
Like a vessel of glass, she stove and sank,
  Ho! ho! the breakers roared!

At daybreak, on the bleak sea-beach,
  A fisherman stood aghast,
To see the form of a maiden fair,
  Lashed close to a drifting mast.

The salt sea was frozen on her breast,
  The salt tears in her eyes;
And he saw her hair, like the brown sea-weed,
  On the billows fall and rise.

Such was the wreck of the Hesperus,
  In the midnight and the snow!
Christ save us all from a death like this,
  On the reef of Norman's Woe!
                    Henry Wadsworth Longfellow.

LORD ULLIN'S DAUGHTER

A CHIEFTAIN, to the Highlands bound,
    Cries: "Boatman, do not tarry!
And I'll give thee a silver pound,
    To row us o'er the ferry!" —

"Now who be ye, would cross Lochgyle,
    This dark and stormy water?"
"Oh, I'm the chief of Ulva's isle,
    And this, Lord Ullin's daughter.

"And fast before her father's men
    Three days we've fled together,
For should he find us in the glen,
    My blood would stain the heather.

"His horsemen hard behind us ride —
    Should they our steps discover,
Then who will cheer my bonny bride,
    When they have slain her lover?"

Out spoke the hardy Highland wight:
    "I'll go, my chief, — I'm ready:
It is not for your silver bright,
    But for your winsome lady: —

"And by my word! the bonny bird
    In danger shall not tarry;

So, though the waves are raging white,
  I'll row you o'er the ferry."

By this the storm grew loud apace,
  The water-wraith was shrieking;
And in the scowl of heaven each face
  Grew dark as they were speaking.

But still, as wilder blew the wind,
  And as the night grew drearer,
Adown the glen rode arméd men,
  Their trampling sounded nearer.

"O haste thee, haste!" the lady cries,
  "Though tempests round us gather;
I'll meet the raging of the skies,
  But not an angry father!"

The boat has left a stormy land,
  A stormy sea before her, —
When, oh! too strong for human hand,
  The tempest gather'd o'er her.

And still they row'd amidst the roar
  Of waters fast prevailing;
Lord Ullin reach'd that fatal shore;
  His wrath was changed to wailing.

For, sore dismay'd, through storm and shade
  His child he did discover;

One lovely hand she stretch'd for aid,
  And one was round her lover.

"Come back! come back!" he cried in grief,
  "Across this stormy water:
And I'll forgive your Highland chief,
  My daughter! — O my daughter!"

'T was vain: the loud waves lash'd the shore,
  Return or aid preventing:
The water wild went o'er his child,
  And he was left lamenting.

Thomas Campbell.

HISTORICAL LEGENDS AND STORIES
(THE CONTINENT, ENGLAND, AND
THE UNITED STATES)

THE LEAK IN THE DIKE

A Story of Holland

The good dame looked from her cottage
  At the close of the pleasant day,
And cheerily called to her little son
  Outside the door at play:
"Come, Peter, come! I want you to go,
  While there is light to see,
To the hut of the blind old man who lives
  Across the dike, for me,
And take these cakes I made for him —
  They are hot and smoking yet;
You have time enough to go and come
  Before the sun is set."

Then the good-wife turned to her labor,
  Humming a simple song,
And thought of her husband, working hard
  At the sluices all day long;
And set the turf a-blazing,
  And brought the coarse black bread;
That he might find a fire at night,
  And find the table spread.

And Peter left the brother
  With whom all day he had played,
And the sister who had watched their sports
  In the willow's tender shade;
And now, with his face all glowing,
  And eyes as bright as the day
With the thoughts of his pleasant errand,
  He trudged along the way;
And soon his joyous prattle
  Made glad a lonesome place.
Alas! if only the blind old man
  Could have seen that happy face!
Yet he somehow caught the brightness
  Which his voice and presence lent;
And he felt the sunshine come and go
  As Peter came and went.

And now, as the day was sinking,
  And the winds began to rise,
The mother looked from her door again,
  Shading her anxious eyes;
And saw the shadows deepen
  And birds to their homes come back,
But never a sign of Peter
  Along the level track.
But she said: "He will come at morning,
  So I need not fret or grieve —
Though it is n't like my boy at all
  To stay without my leave."

But where was the child delaying?
　On the homeward way was he,
And across the dike while the sun was up
　An hour above the sea.
He was stopping now to gather flowers,
　Now listening to the sound,
As the angry waters dashed themselves
　Against their narrow bound.
"Ah! well for us," said Peter,
　"That the gates are good and strong,
And my father tends them carefully,
　Or they would not hold you long!
You're a wicked sea," said Peter;
　"I know why you fret and chafe;
You would like to spoil our lands and homes;
　But our sluices keep you safe!"

But hark! Through the noise of waters
　Comes a low, clear, trickling sound;
And the child's face pales with terror,
　And his blossoms drop to the ground.
He is up the bank in a moment,
　And, stealing through the sand,
He sees a stream not yet so large
　As his slender, childish hand.
'T is a leak in the dike! He is but a boy,
　Unused to fearful scenes;
But, young as he is, he has learned to know,
　The dreadful thing that means.

A leak in the dike! The stoutest heart
　　Grows faint that cry to hear,
And the bravest man in all the land
　　Turns white with mortal fear.
For he knows the smallest leak may grow
　　To a flood in a single night;
And he knows the strength of the cruel sea
　　When loosed in its angry might.

And the boy! He has seen the danger,
　　And, shouting a wild alarm,
He forces back the weight of the sea
　　With the strength of his single arm!
He listens for the joyful sound
　　Of a footstep passing nigh;
And lays his ear to the ground, to catch
　　The answer to his cry.
And he hears the rough winds blowing,
　　And the waters rise and fall,
But never an answer comes to him,
　　Save the echo of his call.
He sees no hope, no succor,
　　His feeble voice is lost;
Yet what shall he do but watch and wait,
　　Though he perish at his post!

So, faintly calling and crying
　　Till the sun is under the sea;

Crying and moaning till the stars
    Come out for company;
He thinks of his brother and sister,
    Asleep in their safe warm bed;
He thinks of his father and mother,
    Of himself as dying — and dead;
And of how, when the night is over,
    They must come and find him at last:
But he never thinks he can leave the place
    Where duty holds him fast.

The good dame in the cottage
    Is up and astir with the light,
For the thought of her little Peter
    Has been with her all night.
And now she watches the pathway,
    As yester eve she had done;
But what does she see so strange and black
    Against the rising sun?
Her neighbors are bearing between them
    Something straight to her door;
Her child is coming home, but not
    As he ever came before!

"He is dead!" she cries; "my darling!"
    And the startled father hears,
And comes and looks the way she looks,
    And fears the thing she fears:

Till a glad shout from the bearers
  Thrills the stricken man and wife:
"Give thanks, for your son has saved our land,
  And God has saved his life!"
So, there in the morning sunshine
  They knelt about the boy;
And every head was bared and bent
  In tearful, reverent joy.

'T is many a year since then; but still,
  When the sea roars like a flood,
Their boys are taught what a boy can do
  Who is brave and true and good.
For every man in that country
  Takes his son by the hand,
And tells him of little Peter,
  Whose courage saved the land.

They have many a valiant hero,
  Remembered through the years:
But never one whose name so oft
  Is named with loving tears.
And his deed shall be sung by the cradle,
  And told to the child on the knee,
So long as the dikes of Holland
  Divide the land from the sea!

(Condensed.) Phœbe Cary.

THE EMPEROR'S BIRD'S–NEST

ONCE the Emperor Charles of Spain,
  With his swarthy, grave commanders,
I forget in what campaign,
Long besieged, in mud and rain,
  Some old frontier town of Flanders.

Up and down the dreary camp,
  In great boots of Spanish leather,
Striding with a measured tramp,
These Hidalgos, dull and damp,
  Cursed the Frenchmen, cursed the weather.

Thus as to and fro they went,
  Over upland and through hollow,
Giving their impatience vent,
Perched upon the Emperor's tent,
  In her nest, they spied a swallow.

Yes, it was a swallow's nest,
  Built of clay and hair of horses,
Mane, or tail, or dragoon's crest,
Found on hedge-rows east and west,
  After skirmish of the forces.

Then an old Hidalgo said,
  As he twirled his gray mustachio:

"Sure this swallow overhead
Thinks the Emperor's tent a shed,
  And the Emperor but a Macho!"

Hearing his imperial name
  Coupled with those words of malice,
Half in anger, half in shame,
Forth the great campaigner came
  Slowly from his canvas palace.

"Let no hand the bird molest,"
  Said he solemnly, "nor hurt her!"
Adding then, by way of jest,
"Golondrina is my guest,
  'T is the wife of some deserter!"

Swift as bowstring speeds a shaft,
  Through the camp was spread the rumor,
And the soldiers, as they quaffed
Flemish beer at dinner, laughed
  At the Emperor's pleasant humor.

So unharmed and unafraid
  Sat the swallow still and brooded,
Till the constant cannonade
Through the walls a breach had made
  And the siege was thus concluded.

Then the army, elsewhere bent,
  Struck its tents as if disbanding,

Only not the Emperor's tent,
For he ordered, ere he went,
  Very curtly: "Leave it standing!"

So it stood there all alone,
  Loosely flapping, torn and tattered,
Till the brood was fledged and flown,
Singing o'er those walls of stone
  Which the cannon-shot had shattered.

Henry Wadsworth Longfellow.

THE NIBELUNGEN TREASURE

It was an ancient monarch
  Ruled where the Rhine doth flow,
And nought he loved so little
  As sorrow, feud, and woe;
His warriors they were striving
  For a treasure in the land;
In sooth they near had perished
  Each by his brother's hand.

Then spake he to the nobles:
  "What boots this gold," he said,
"If with the finder's life-blood
  The price thereof is paid?
The gold, to end the quarrel,
  Cast to the Rhine away;

There lie the treasure hidden,
Till dawns the latest day!"

The proud ones took the treasure,
And cast it to the main;
I ween it all hath melted,
So long it there hath lain:
But, wedded to the waters
That long have o'er it rolled,
It clothes the swelling vineyards
With yellow gleam, like gold.

Oh, that each man were minded,
As thought this monarch good,
That never care might alter
His high, courageous mood!
Then deeply would we bury
Our sorrows in the Rhine,
And, glad of heart and grateful,
Would quaff his fiery wine.

From the German.
Translated by H. W. Dulcken.

BARBAROSSA

THE ancient Barbarossa
By magic spell is bound, —
Old Frederic the Kaiser,
In castle underground.

The Kaiser hath not perished,
  He sleeps an iron sleep;
For, in the castle hidden,
  He's sunk in slumber deep.

With him the chiefest treasures
  Of empire hath he ta'en,
Wherewith, in fitting season,
  He shall appear again.

The Kaiser he is sitting
  Upon an ivory throne;
Of marble is the table
  His head he resteth on.

His beard it is not flaxen,
  Like a living fire it shines,
And groweth through the table
  Whereon his chin reclines.

As in a dream he noddeth,
  Then wakes he, heavy-eyed,
And calls, with lifted finger,
  A stripling to his side.

"Dwarf, get thee to the gateway,
  And tidings bring, if still
Their course the ancient ravens
  Are wheeling round the hill.

"For if the ancient ravens
Are flying still around,
A hundred years to slumber
By magic spell I'm bound."

From the German of Friedrich Rückert.
Translated by H. W. Dulcken.

THE RICHEST PRINCE

ALL their wealth and vast possessions
Vaunting high in choicest terms,
Sat the German princes feasting
In the knightly hall of Worms.

"Mighty," cried the Saxon ruler,
"Are the wealth and power I wield:
In my country's mountain gorges
Sparkling silver lies concealed."

"See my land with plenty glowing,"
Quoth the Palsgrave of the Rhine;
"Beauteous harvests in the valleys,
On the mountains noble wine."

"Spacious towns and wealthy convents,"
Lewis spake, Bavaria's lord,
"Make my land to yield me treasures
Great as those your fields afford."

Würtemberg's belovéd monarch,
  Eberhard the Bearded, cried:
"See, my land hath little cities,
  'Mong my hills no metals bide;

"Yet one treasure it hath borne me, —
  Sleeping in the woodland free,
I may lay my head in safety
  On my lowliest vassal's knee."

Then, as with a single utterance,
  Cried aloud those princes three:
"Bearded count, thy land hath jewels!
  Thou art wealthier far than we!"

From the German of Andreas J. Kerner.
Translated by H. W. Dulcken.

THE BATTLE OF BLENHEIM

(August 13, 1704)

It was a summer evening,
  Old Kaspar's work was done,
And he before his cottage door
  Was sitting in the sun;
And by him sported on the green
His little grandchild Wilhelmine.

She saw her brother Peterkin
  Roll something large and round,

Which he, beside the rivulet,
  In playing there, had found;
He came to ask what he had found,
  That was so large, and smooth, and round.

Old Kaspar took it from the boy,
  Who stood expectant by;
And then the old man shook his head,
  And, with a natural sigh,
"'T is some poor fellow's skull," said he,
"Who fell in the great victory!

"I find them in the garden,
  For there's many here about;
And often when I go to plough,
  The ploughshare turns them out!
For many thousand men," said he,
"Were slain in that great victory!"

"Now tell us what 't was all about,"
  Young Peterkin he cries;
And little Wilhelmine looks up
  With wonder-waiting eyes;
"Now tell us all about the war,
And what they killed each other for."

"It was the English," Kaspar cried,
  "Who put the French to rout;
But what they fought each other for,
  I could not well make out;

But everybody said," quoth he,
"That 't was a famous victory.

"My father lived at Blenheim then,
    Yon little stream hard by;
They burned his dwelling to the ground,
    And he was forced to fly;
So with his wife and child he fled,
Nor had he where to rest his head.

"With fire and sword the country round
    Was wasted far and wide;
And many a childing mother then
    And new-born baby died;
But things like that, you know, must be
At every famous victory.

"They say it was a shocking sight
    After the field was won;
For many thousand bodies here
    Lay rotting in the sun.
But things like that, you know, must be
After a famous victory.

"Great praise the Duke of Marlboro' won,
    And our good Prince Eugene."
"Why, 't was a very wicked thing!"
    Said little Wilhelmine.
"Nay, nay, my little girl," quoth he,
"It was a famous victory!

"And everybody praised the Duke
  Who this great fight did win."
"But what good came of it at last?"
  Quoth little Peterkin.
"Why that I cannot tell," said he,
"But 't was a famous victory."

Robert Southey.

NAPOLEON AND THE ENGLISH SAILOR BOY

I LOVE contemplating — apart
  From all his homicidal glory —
The traits that soften to our heart
  Napoleon's story.

'T was when his banners at Boulogne
  Armed in our island every freeman;
His navy chanced to capture one
  Poor British seaman.

They suffered him — I know not how —
  Unprisoned on the shore to roam;
And aye was bent his longing brow
  On England's home.

His eye, methinks, pursued the flight
  Of birds to Britain half-way over

With envy, — *they* could reach the white,
  Dear cliffs of Dover.

A stormy midnight watch, he thought,
  Than this sojourn would have been dearer,
If but the storm his vessel brought
  To England nearer.

At last, when care had banished sleep,
  He saw one morning — dreaming — doting,
An empty hogshead from the deep
  Come shoreward floating.

He hid it in a cave, and wrought
  The livelong day laborious, lurking,
Until he launched a tiny boat
  By mighty working.

Heaven help us! 't was a thing beyond
  Description wretched: such a wherry
Perhaps ne'er ventured on a pond,
  Or crossed a ferry.

For ploughing in the salt sea field,
  It would have made the boldest shudder;
Untarred, uncompassed, and unkeeled,
  No sail — no rudder.

From neighboring woods he interlaced
  His sorry skiff with wattled willows;

And thus equipped he would have passed
  The foaming billows.

But Frenchmen caught him on the beach,
  His little Argo sorely jeering;
Till tidings of him chanced to reach
  Napoleon's hearing.

With folded arms Napoleon stood,
  Serene alike in peace and danger,
And in his wonted attitude
  Addressed the stranger:

"Rash man, that wouldst yon channel pass
  On twigs and staves so rudely fashioned!
Thy heart with some sweet British lass
  Must be impassioned."

"I have no sweetheart," said the lad;
  "But, absent long from one another,
Great was the longing that I had
  To see my mother."

"And so thou shalt!" Napoleon said;
  "Ye've both my favor fairly won:
A noble mother must have bred
  So brave a son."

He gave the tar a piece of gold,
  And with a flag of truce commanded

He should be shipped to England Old,
  And safely landed.

Our sailor oft could scantily shift
  To find a dinner plain and hearty;
But never changed the coin and gift
  Of Bonaparté.

Thomas Campbell.

INCIDENT OF THE FRENCH CAMP

You know, we French stormed Ratisbon; —
  A mile or so away,
On a little mound, Napoleon
  Stood on our storming day;
With neck out-thrust, you fancy how,
  Legs wide, arms locked behind,
As if to balance the prone brow
  Oppressive with its mind.

Just as perhaps he mused: "My plans
  That soar, to earth may fall,
Let once my army-leader Lannes
  Waver at yonder wall," —
Out 'twixt the battery-smokes there flew
  A rider, bound on bound
Full-galloping; nor bridle drew
  Until he reached the mound.

Then off there flung in smiling joy,
  And held himself erect
By just his horse's mane, a boy:
  You hardly could suspect —
(So tight he kept his lips compressed,
  Scarce any blood came through,)
You looked twice e'er you saw his breast
  Was all but shot in two.

"Well," cried he, "Emperor, by God's grace
  We've got you Ratisbon!
The marshal's in the market-place,
  And you'll be there anon
To see your flag-bird flap his vans
  Where I, to heart's desire,
Perched him." The chief's eye flashed; his
    plans
  Soared up again like fire.

The chief's eye flashed; but presently
  Softened itself, as sheathes
A film the mother eagle's eye
  When her bruised eaglet breathes:
"You're wounded!" "Nay," his soldier's
    pride
  Touched to the quick, he said;
"I'm killed, sire!" And, his chief beside,
  Smiling, the boy fell dead.

Robert Browning.

KING CANUTE

King Canute was weary hearted; he had
    reigned for years a score,
Battling, struggling, pushing, fighting, killing
    much, and robbing more;
And he thought upon his actions, walking by
    the wild sea-shore.

'Twixt the Chancellor and the Bishop, walked
    the King with steps sedate,
Chamberlains and grooms came after, silver-
    sticks and gold-sticks great,
Chaplains, aides-de-camp and pages, — all the
    officers of state.

Sliding after like his shadow, pausing when he
    chose to pause,
If a frown his face contracted, straight the
    courtiers dropped their jaws;
If to laugh the King was minded, out they
    burst in loud hee-haws.

But that day a something vexed him; that
    was clear to old and young;
Thrice His Grace had yawned at table when
    his favorite gleemen sung,
Once the Queen would have consoled him, but
    he bade her hold her tongue.

"Something ails my gracious master!" cried
    the Keeper of the Seal,
"Sure, my lord, it is the lampreys served for
    dinner, or the veal?"
"Psha!" exclaimed the angry monarch,
    "Keeper, 't is not that I feel.

"'T is the *heart*, and not the dinner, fool, that
    doth my rest impair;
Can a king be great as I am, prithee, and yet
    know no care?
Oh, I'm sick, and tired, and weary." Some
    one cried: "The King's arm-chair!"

Then toward the lackeys turning, quick my
    Lord the Keeper nodded,
Straight the King's great chair was brought
    him, by two footmen able-bodied;
Languidly he sank into it; it was comfortably
    wadded.

"Nay, I feel," replied King Canute, "that my
    end is drawing near."
"Don't say so!" exclaimed the courtiers (striv-
    ing each to squeeze a tear).
"Sure your Grace is strong and lusty, and
    may live this fifty year!"

"Live these fifty years!" the Bishop roared,
    with actions made to suit.

"Are you mad, my good Lord Keeper, thus
    to speak of King Canute!
Men have lived a thousand years, and sure
    His Majesty will do't.

"With his wondrous skill in healing ne'er a
    doctor can compete,
Loathsome lepers, if he touch them, start up
    clean upon their feet;
Surely he could raise the dead up, did His
    Highness think it meet.

"Did not once the Jewish captain stay the
    sun upon the hill,
And the while he slew the foemen, bid the
    silver moon stand still?
So, no doubt, could gracious Canute, if it were
    his sacred will."

"Might I stay the sun above us, good Sir
    Bishop?" Canute cried,
"Could I bid the silver moon to pause upon
    her heavenly ride?
If the moon obeys my orders, sure I can com-
    mand the tide!

"Will the advancing waves obey me, Bishop,
    if I make the sign?"
Said the Bishop, bowing lowly: "Land and
    sea, my Lord, are thine."

Canute turned toward the ocean: "Back!" he
    said, "thou foaming brine.

"From the sacred shore I stand on, I command
    thee to retreat;
Venture not, thou stormy rebel, to approach
    thy master's seat;
Ocean, be thou still! I bid thee come not
    nearer to my feet!"

But the sullen ocean answered with a louder,
    deeper roar,
And the rapid waves drew nearer, falling
    sounding on the shore;
Back the Keeper and the Bishop, back the King
    and courtiers bore.

And he sternly bade them never more to kneel
    to human clay,
But alone to praise and worship That which
    earth and seas obey;
And his golden crown of empire never wore he
    from that day.

(*Condensed.*) *William Makepeace Thackeray.*

KING EDWIN'S FEAST

There was feasting in the hall
And the beards wagged all.

Oh! the board was heaped with food,
And the ale was like a flood,
  And 't was bitter winter weather
When King Edwin and his Eldormen and
    Thanes
  Were a-feasting thus together.

As the board was heaped with food,
So the hearth was piled with wood;
Ay, with oaken logs a score;
And the flames did leap and roar.
  And they cast a ruddy glow
On King Edwin and his Eldormen and Thanes
  As they feasted in a row.

All at once they were aware
Of a flutter in the air,
As a little sparrow came
In between them and the flame,
  Then a moment flew around,
While King Edwin and his Eldormen and
    Thanes
  Wondered whither he was bound.

Then he vanished through the door,
And they never saw him more;
But up spoke a noble Thane,
As a silence seemed to reign,
  And a wonder seemed to fall

On King Edwin and his Eldormen and Thanes
  As they feasted in the hall:

"What is all this life of ours,
With its graces and its powers?
It is like the bird that came
In between us and the flame,
  Stayed a moment in the room
With King Edwin and his Eldormen and
    Thanes,
    Then was off into the gloom.

"So we come out of the night,
Stay a moment in the light
Of a warm and pleasant room,
Then go forth into the gloom;
  Hither somehow tempest-tost,
O King Edwin! and you, Eldormen and
    Thanes,
    Then again in darkness lost."

Then another silence fell
And the first who broke the spell
Was Paulinius, the Christian, and he said,
Bowing low a reverent head
  That was white with many years,
To King Edwin and his Eldormen and
    Thanes,
    And his words were dim with tears:

"Oh! not merely tempest-tost,
Not again in darkness lost,
Is the little bird that came
In between us and the flame;
  For the bird will find his nest.
So, King Edwin, and you, Eldormen and
      Thanes,
    Be not your hearts distressed.

"Not from darkness comes the soul,
Nor shall darkness be its goal.
For that, too, there is a nest,
Whither flying it shall rest
    Evermore. It must be so."
Said King Edwin and his Eldormen and
      Thanes:
  "Would to God that we might know!"
                    John W. Chadwick.

KING ALFRED THE HARPER

Dark fell the night, the watch was set,
The host was idly spread,
The Danes around their watchfires met,
Caroused, and fiercely fed.

The chiefs beneath a tent of leaves,
And Guthrum, king of all,

Devoured the flesh of England's beeves,
And laughed at England's fall.
Each warrior proud, each Danish earl,
In mail and wolf-skin clad,
Their bracelets white with plundered pearl,
Their eyes with triumph mad.

In stalked a warrior tall and rude
Before the strong sea-kings:
"Ye Lords and Earls of Odin's brood,
Without a Harper sings.
He seems a simple man and poor,
But well he sounds the lay;
And well, ye Norsemen chiefs, be sure,
Will ye the song repay!"

In trod the bard with keen cold look,
And glanced along the board,
That with the shout and war-cry shook
Of many a Danish lord.
But thirty brows, inflamed and stern,
Soon bent on him their gaze,
While calm he gazed, as if to learn
Who chief deserved his praise.

Loud Guthrum spake:—"Nay, gaze not thus,
Thou Harper weak and poor!
By Thor! who bandy looks with us
Must worse than looks endure.

Sing high the praise of Denmark's host,
High praise each dauntless Earl;
The brave who stun this English coast
With war's unceasing whirl."

The Harper slowly bent his head,
And touched aloud the string;
Then raised his face, and boldly said:
"Hear thou my lay, O King!
High praise from every mouth of man
To all who boldly strive,
Who fall where first the fight began,
And ne'er go back alive.

"Fill high your cups, and swell the shout,
At famous Regnar's name!
Who sank his host in bloody rout,
When he to Humber came.
His men were chased, his sons were slain,
And he was left alone.
They bound him in an iron chain
Upon a dungeon stone.
With iron links they bound him fast;
With snakes they filled the hole,
That made his flesh their long repast,
And bit into his soul.

"Great Chiefs, why sink in gloom your eyes?
Why champ your teeth in pain?

Still lives the song though Regnar dies!
Fill high your cups again.
Ye too, perchance, O Norsemen lords!
Who fought and swayed so long,
Shall soon but live in minstrel words,
And owe your names to song.

"This land has graves by thousands more
Than that where Regnar lies.
When conquests fade, and rule is o'er,
The sod must close your eyes.
How soon, who knows? Not chief, nor bard;
And yet to me 't is given,
To see your foreheads deeply scarred,
And guess the doom of Heaven.

"I may not read or when or how,
But, Earls and Kings, be sure
I see a blade o'er every brow,
Where pride now sits secure.
Fill high the cups, raise loud the strain!
When chief and monarch fall,
Their names in song shall breathe again,
And thrill the feastful hall."

Grim sat the chiefs; one heaved a groan,
And one grew pale with dread,
His iron mace was grasped by one,
By one his wine was shed.

And Guthrum cried: "Nay, bard, no more
We hear thy boding lay;
Make drunk the song with spoil and gore!
Light up the joyous fray!"

"Quick throbs my brain," — so burst the
      song, —
"To hear the strife once more.
The mace, the axe, they rest too long;
Earth cries, 'My thirst is sore!'
More blithely twang the strings of bows
Than strings of harps in glee;
Red wounds are lovelier than the rose,
Or rosy lips to me.

"Oh! fairer than a field of flowers,
When flowers in England grew,
Would be the battle's marshalled powers,
The plain of carnage new.
With all its deaths before my soul
The vision rises fair;
Raise loud the song, and drain the bowl!
I would that I were there!"

Loud rang the harp, the minstrel's eye
Rolled fiercely round the throng;
It seemed two crashing hosts were nigh,
Whose shock aroused the song.

A golden cup King Guthrum gave
To him who strongly played;
And said: "I won it from the slave
Who once o'er England swayed."

King Guthrum cried: "'T was Alfred's own;
Thy song befits the brave:
The King who cannot guard his throne
Nor wine nor song shall have!"
The minstrel took the goblet bright,
And said: "I drink the wine
To him who owns by justest right
The cup thou bid'st be mine.
To him, your Lord, Oh, shout ye all!
His meed be deathless praise!
The King who dares not nobly fall,
Dies basely all his days."

"The praise thou speakest," Guthrum said,
"With sweetness fills mine ear;
For Alfred swift before me fled,
And left me monarch here.
The royal coward never dared
Beneath mine eye to stand.
Oh, would that now this feast he shared,
And saw me rule his land!"

Then stern the minstrel rose, and spake,
And gazed upon the King, —

"Not now the golden cup I take,
Nor more to thee I sing.
Another day, a happier hour,
Shall bring me here again:
The cup shall stay in Guthrum's power
Till I demand it then."

The Harper turned and left the shed,
Nor bent to Guthrum's crown;
And one who marked his visage said
It wore a ghastly frown.
The Danes ne'er saw that Harper more,
For soon as morning rose,
Upon their camp *King Alfred* bore,
And slew ten thousand foes.

(Condensed.) John Sterling.

TAILLEFER THE MINSTREL

DUKE WILLIAM the Norman spake out one
        day:
"Who sings in my court and my room alway?
Who sings from the morning till late at night,
So sweetly, my heart seems to laugh out-
        right?"

"'T is Taillefer, my liege, that so sweetly sings,
In the court, as the windlass around he swings,

In the room, as the fire he fans and rakes,
When at eve he lies down, and at morn
    awakes."

"'T is well," quoth the Duke, "I've a servant
    rare
In Taillefer, who serves me with faith and
    care.
The wheel he turns and the fire makes bright,
And so clearly he sings that my heart grows
    light."

Then Taillefer answered: "Were I but *free*,
Far better I'd labor and sing for thee!
How well on horseback I'd serve my lord,
And sing, as I clashed my shield and sword!"

Soon Taillefer rode to the battle-field
On a war-horse stout, with sword and shield;
Duke William's sister, as down she gazed
From a turret, the knight's bold bearing
    praised.

And when 'neath her turret he rode, he sang;
Like a breeze, and next like a storm it rang;
She cried: "When he singeth, what joys
    awake!
The tower is shaken, my heart doth quake!"

  .   .   .   .

Duke William sailed with a mighty host
O'er the rolling billows to England's coast.
He sprang from the ship — on his hands he
        fell:
"Ha! England!" he shouted, "I grasp thee
        well!"

As the Norman host to the battle strode,
For a boon, to the Duke brave Taillefer rode.
"Many years have I sung, while thy fire I
        made,
Many years, while the sword and the lance
        I've swayed.

"If I've served thee and sung to thy heart's
        delight,
At first as a servant, and last as a knight,
Then grant me this boon — when the morn
        shall shine,
Let the first blow struck at the foe be mine!"

With sword and spear he his horse bestrode,
Before the whole army brave Taillefer rode;
Over Hastings' field his song rang out,
Of Roland he sang, and of heroes stout.

When the "Roland-Song" rose loud as a
        blast,
Many standards waved, many hearts beat
        fast;

Its notes with courage the knights inspire:
For well, as he sang, could he *fan their fire!*

Then, charging, his first quick thrust he gave,
An English knight to the ground he drave;
His sword he swung for the first swift blow,
An English knight on the ground lay low.

The Normans beheld it, and stayed not long;
With yells and smiting of shields they
    throng;
Hark! arrows are whirring, swords clash in the
    fray,
Till Harold is slain and his host gives way.

The Duke on the field his standard spread,
His tent he pitched i' the midst o' the dead;
A golden beaker his table graced,
And the English crown on his head was
    placed.

"Come, pledge me, my Taillefer brave, this
    day!
In love and in grief thou hast tuned thy lay,
But on Hastings' field thou hast sung me a
    song
Shall ring in my ears for my whole life long!"

From the German of Ludwig Uhland.
Translated by W. W. Skeat.

THE RELIEF OF LUCKNOW

Oh, that last day in Lucknow fort!
  We knew that it was the last;
That the enemy's lines crept surely on,
  And the end was coming fast.

To yield to that foe meant worse than death;
  And the men and we all worked on;
It was one day more of smoke and roar,
  And then it would all be done.

There was one of us, a corporal's wife,
  A fair, young, gentle thing,
Wasted with fever in the siege,
  And her mind was wandering.

She lay on the ground, in her Scottish plaid,
  And I took her head on my knee;
"When my father comes hame frae the
      pleugh," she said,
  "Oh, then please wauken me."

She slept like a child on her father's floor,
  In the flecking of woodbine-shade,
When the house-dog sprawls by the open
      door,
  And the mother's wheel is stayed.

It was smoke and roar and powder-stench,
   And hopeless waiting for death;
And the soldier's wife, like a full-tired child,
   Seemed scarce to draw her breath.

I sank to sleep; and I had my dream
   Of an English village-lane,
And wall and garden; — but one wild scream
   Brought me back to the roar again.

There Jessie Brown stood listening
   Till a sudden gladness broke
All over her face; and she caught my hand
   And drew me near as she spoke: —

"The Hielanders! Oh! dinna ye hear
   The slogan far awa'?
The McGregor's. Oh! I ken it weel;
   It's the grandest o' them a'!

"God bless the bonny Hielanders!
   We're saved! we're saved!" she cried;
And fell on her knees; and thanks to God
   Flowed forth like a full flood-tide.

Along the battery-line her cry
   Had fallen among the men,
And they started back; — they were there to
      die;
   But was life so near them, then?

They listened for life; the rattling fire
  Far off, and the far-off roar,
Were all; and the colonel shook his head,
  And they turned to their guns once more.

But Jessie said: "The slogan's done;
  But winna ye hear it noo?
'The Campbells are comin'"? It's no a dream;
  Our succors hae broken through!"

We heard the roar and the rattle afar,
  But the pipes we could not hear;
So the men plied their work of hopeless war,
  And knew that the end was near.

It was not long ere it made its way, —
  A thrilling, ceaseless sound:
It was no noise from the strife afar,
  Or the sappers under ground.

It *was* the pipes of the Highlanders!
  And now they played "Auld Lang Syne."
It came to our men like the voice of God,
  And they shouted along the line.

And they wept, and shook one another's
      hands,
  And the women sobbed in a crowd;
And every one knelt down where he stood,
  And we all thanked God aloud.

That happy time, when we welcomed them,
  Our men put Jessie first;
And the general gave her his hand, and cheers
  Like a storm from the soldiers burst.

And the pipers' ribbons and tartan streamed,
  Marching round and round our line;
And our joyful cheers were broken with tears,
  As the pipes played "Auld Lang Syne."

Robert Traill Spence Lowell.

THE FOUNTAIN OF YOUTH

I

A STORY of Ponce de Leon,
  A voyager, withered and old,
Who came to the sunny Antilles,
  In quest of a country of gold.
He was wafted past islands of spices,
  As bright as the emerald seas,
Where all the forests seem singing,
  So thick were the birds on the trees.
There came to De Leon, the sailor,
  Some Indian sages, who told
Of a region so bright that the waters
  Were sprinkled with islands of gold.
And they added: "The leafy Bimini,
  A fair land of grottos and bowers,

And his anchor he lifted and murmured, —
  As the tears gathered fast in his eye:
"I must leave this fair land of the flowers,
  Go back o'er the ocean, and die."
Then back by the dreary Tortugas,
  And back by the shady Azores,
He was borne on the storm-smitten waters
  To the calm of his own native shores.
And that he grew older and older,
  His footsteps enfeebled gave proof,
Still he thirsted in dreams for the foun-
     tain, —
  The beautiful Fountain of Youth.

  .   .   .   .

v

One day the old sailor lay dying
  On the shores of a tropical isle,
And his heart was enkindled with rapture,
  And his face lighted up with a smile.
He thought of the sunny Antilles,
  He thought of the shady Azores,
He thought of the dreamy Bahamas,
  He thought of fair Florida's shores,
And when in his mind he passed over
  His wonderful travels of old,
He thought of the heavenly country,
  Of the city of jasper and gold.

"Thank the Lord!" said De Leon, the sailor,
  "Thank the Lord for the light of the
    truth,
I now am approaching the fountain, —
  The beautiful Fountain of Youth."

VI

The cabin was silent: at twilight
  They heard the birds singing a psalm,
And the wind of the ocean low sighing
  Through groves of the orange and palm.
The sailor still lay on his pallet,
  'Neath the low-hanging vines of the
    roof;
His soul had gone forth to discover
  The beautiful Fountain of Youth.

(Condensed.) Hezekiah Butterworth.

QUIVIRA

FRANCISCO CORONADO rode forth with all his
    train,
Eight hundred savage bowmen, three hundred
    spears of Spain,
To seek the rumored glory that pathless
    deserts hold, —
The City of Quivira whose walls are rich with
    gold.

Oh, gay they rode with plume on crest and
    gilded spur at heel,
With gonfalon of Aragon and banner of Castile!
While High Emprise and Joyous Youth, twin
    marshals of the throng,
Awoke Sonora's mountain peaks with trum-
    pet-note and song.

Beside that brilliant army, beloved of serf
    and lord,
There walked as brave a soldier as ever smote
    with sword,
Though nought of knightly harness his russet
    gown revealed —
The cross he bore as weapon, the missal was
    his shield.

But rugged oaths were changed to prayers,
    and angry hearts grew tame,
And fainting spirits waxed in faith where
    Fray Padilla came;
And brawny spearmen bowed their heads to
    kiss the helpful hand
Of him who spake the simple truth that brave
    men understand.

What pen may paint their daring — those
    doughty cavaliers!
The cities of the Zuñi were humbled by their
    spears.

Wild Arizona's barrens grew pallid in the glow
Of blades that won Granada and conquered
    Mexico.

They fared by lofty Acoma; their rally-call
    was blown
Where Colorado rushes down through God-
    hewn walls of stone;
Still, North and East, where deserts spread,
    and treeless prairies rolled,
A Fairy City lured them on with pinnacles of
    gold.

Through all their weary marches toward that
    flitting goal
They turned to Fray Padilla for aid of heart
    and soul.
He bound the wounds that lance-thrust and
    flinty arrow made;
He cheered the sick and failing; above the
    dead he prayed.

Two thousand miles of war and woe behind
    their banners lay:
And sadly fever, drought and toil had lessened
    their array,
When came a message fraught with hope to
    all the steadfast band:
"Good tidings from the northward, friends!
    Quivira lies at hand!"

How joyously they spurred them! How sadly
    drew the rein!
There shone no golden palace, there blazed no
    jeweled fane.
Rude tents of hide of bison, dog-guarded, met
    their view —
A squalid Indian village; the lodges of the Sioux!

Then Coronado bowed his head. He spake
    unto his men:
"Our quest is vain, true hearts of Spain! Now
    ride we home again.
And would to God that I might give that
    phantom city's pride
In ransom for the gallant souls that here have
    sunk and died!"

Back, back to Compostela the wayworn
    handful bore:
But sturdy Fray Padilla took up the quest
    once more.
His soul still longed for conquest, though not
    by lance and sword;
He burned to show the Heathen the pathway
    to the Lord.

Again he trudged the flinty hills and dazzling
    desert sands,
And few were they that walked with him, and
    weaponless their hands —

But and the trusty man-at-arms, Docampo,
    rode him near
Like Great Heart guarding Christian's way
    through wastes of Doubt and Fear.

Where still in silken harvests the prairie-lilies
    toss,
Among the dark Quiviras Padilla reared his
    cross.
Within its sacred shadow the warriors of the Kaw
In wonder heard the Gospel of Love and
    Peace and Law.

They gloried in their Brown-robed Priest;
    and oft in twilight's gold
The warriors grouped, a silent ring, to hear
    the tale he told;
While round the gentle man-at-arms their
    lithe-limbed children played
And shot their arrows at his shield and rode
    his guarded blade.

When thrice the silver crescent had filled its
    curving shell,
The Friar rose at dawning and spake his flock
    farewell:
"— And if your Brothers northward be cruel,
    as ye say,
My Master bids me seek them — and dare I
    answer 'Nay'?"

Again he strode the path of thorns; but ere
     the evening star
A savage cohort swept the plain in paint and
     plumes of war.
Then Fray Padilla spake to them whose hearts
     were most his own:
"My children, bear the tidings home — let
     me die here alone."

He knelt upon the prairie, begirt by yelling
     Sioux. —
"Forgive them, oh, my Father! they know not
     what they do!"
The twanging bow-strings answered. Before
     his eyes, unrolled
The City of Quivira whose streets are paved
     with gold.

Arthur Guiterman.

POCAHONTAS

Wearied arm and broken sword
     Wage in vain the desperate fight;
Round him press a countless horde,
     He is but a single knight.
Hark! a cry of triumph shrill
     Through the wilderness resounds,
     As, with twenty bleeding wounds,
Sinks the warrior, fighting still.

Now they heap the funeral pyre,
    And the torch of death they light;
Ah! 't is hard to die of fire!
    Who will shield the captive knight?
Round the stake with fiendish cry
    Wheel and dance the savage crowd,
    Cold the victim's mien and proud,
And his breast is bared to die.

Who will shield the fearless heart?
    Who avert the murderous blade?
From the throng with sudden start
    See, there springs an Indian maid.
Quick she stands before the knight:
    "Loose the chain, unbind the ring!
    I am daughter of the king,
And I claim the Indian right!"

Dauntlessly aside she flings
    Lifted axe and thirsty knife,
Fondly to his heart she clings,
    And her bosom guards his life!
In the woods of Powhatan,
    Still 't is told by Indian fires
    How a daughter of their sires
Saved a captive Englishman.
                    William Makepeace Thackeray.

THE FIRST THANKSGIVING DAY

(*November, 1621*)

"AND now," said the Governor, gazing abroad
    on the piled-up store
Of the sheaves that dotted the clearings and
    covered the meadows o'er,
"'T is meet that we render praises because of
    this yield of grain;
'T is meet that the Lord of the harvest be
    thanked for His sun and rain.

"And therefore I, William Bradford (by the
    grace of God to-day,
And the franchise of this good people), Gov-
    ernor of Plymouth, say,
Through virtue of vested power — ye shall
    gather with one accord,
And hold, in the month November, thanksgiv-
    ing unto the Lord.

"He hath granted us peace and plenty, and
    the quiet we've sought so long;
He hath thwarted the wily savage, and kept
    him from wrack and wrong;
And unto our feast the Sachem shall be bid-
    den, that he may know
We worship his own Great Spirit who maketh
    the harvest grow.

"So shoulder your matchlocks, masters: there
    is hunting of all degrees;
And fishermen, take your tackle, and scour
    for spoil the seas;
And maidens and dames of Plymouth, your
    delicate crafts employ
To honor our First Thanksgiving, and make
    it a feast of joy!

"We fail of the fruits and dainties — we fail
    of the old home cheer;
Ah, these are the lightest losses, mayhap, that
    befall us here;
But see, in our open clearings, how golden the
    melons lie;
Enrich them with sweets and spices, and give
    us the pumpkin-pie!"

So, bravely the preparations went on for the
    autumn feast;
The deer and the bear were slaughtered; wild
    game from the greatest to least
Was heaped in the colony cabins; brown
    home-brew served for wine,
And the plum and the grape of the forest, for
    orange and peach and pine.

At length came the day appointed: the snow
    had begun to fall,
But the clang from the meeting-house belfry
    rang merrily over all,

And summoned the folk of Plymouth, who
    hastened with glad accord
To listen to Elder Brewster as he fervently
    thanked the Lord.

In his seat sat Governor Bradford; men,
    matrons, and maidens fair;
Miles Standish and all his soldiers, with
    corselet and sword, were there;
And sobbing and tears and gladness had each
    in its turn the sway,
For the grave of the sweet Rose Standish
    o'ershadowed Thanksgiving Day.

And when Massasoit, the Sachem, sate down
    with his hundred braves,
And ate of the varied riches of gardens and
    woods and waves,
And looked on the granaried harvest, — with
    a blow on his brawny chest,
He muttered: "The good Great Spirit loves
    His white children best!"

                Margaret Junkin Preston.

RODNEY'S RIDE

(July 3, 1776)

In that soft mid-land where the breezes bear
The North and the South on the genial air,

Through the county of Kent, on affairs of state,
Rode Cæsar Rodney, the delegate.

Burly and big, and bold and bluff,
In his three-cornered hat and coat of snuff,
A foe to King George and the English State,
Was Cæsar Rodney, the delegate.

Into Dover village he rode apace,
And his kinsfolk knew, from his anxious face,
It was matter grave that brought him there,
To the counties three on the Delaware.

"Money and men we must have," he said,
"Or the Congress fails and our cause is dead;
Give us both and the King shall not work his
    will.
We are men, since the blood of Bunker Hill!"

Comes a rider swift on a panting bay:
"Ho, Rodney, ho! you must save the day,
For the Congress halts at a deed so great,
And your vote alone may decide its fate."

Answered Rodney then: "I will ride with
    speed;
It is Liberty's stress; it is Freedom's need.
When stands it?" "To-night. Not a moment
    to spare,
But ride like the wind from the Delaware."

"Ho, saddle the black! I've but half a day,
And the Congress sits eighty miles away —·
And I'll be in time, if God grants me grace,
To shake my fist in King George's face."

He is up; he is off! and the black horse flies
On the northward road ere the "God-speed"
          dies;
It is gallop and spur, as the leagues they clear,
And the clustering mile-stones move a-rear.

It is two of the clock; and the fleet hoofs fling
The Fieldboro's dust with a clang and a cling;
It is three; and he gallops with slack rein
          where
The road winds down to the Delaware.

Four; and he spurs into New Castle town,
From his panting steed he gets him down —
"A fresh one, quick! not a moment's wait!"
And off speeds Rodney, the delegate.

It is five; and the beams of the western sun
Tinge the spires of Wilmington gold and dun;
Six; and the dust of Chester Street
Flies back in a cloud from the courser's feet.

It is seven; the horse-boat broad of beam,
At the Schuylkill ferry crawls over the
          stream —

And at seven-fifteen by the Rittenhouse clock,
He flings his reins to the tavern jock.

The Congress is met; the debate 's begun,
And Liberty lags for the vote of one —
When into the hall, not a moment late,
Walks Cæsar Rodney, the delegate.

Not a moment late! and that half day's ride
Forwards the world with a mighty stride;
For the act was passed; ere the midnight
    stroke
O'er the Quaker City its echoes woke.

At Tyranny's feet was the gauntlet flung;
"We are free!" all the bells through the
    colonies rung.
And the sons of the free may recall with pride
The day of Delegate Rodney's ride.

Elbridge Streeter Brooks.

PAUL REVERE'S RIDE

LISTEN, my children, and you shall hear
Of the midnight ride of Paul Revere,
On the eighteenth of April, in Seventy-five;
Hardly a man is now alive
Who remembers that famous day and year.

He said to his friend: "If the British march
By land or sea from the town to-night,
Hang a lantern aloft in the belfry-arch
Of the North Church tower as a signal light, —
One, if by land, and two, if by sea;
And I on the opposite shore will be,
Ready to ride and spread the alarm
Through every Middlesex village and farm,
For the country folk to be up and to arm."

Then he said: "Good night!" and with muffled
          oar
Silently rowed to the Charlestown shore,
Just as the moon rose over the bay,
Where swinging wide at her moorings lay
The Somerset, British man-of-war;
A phantom ship, with each mast and spar
Across the moon like a prison bar,
And a huge black hulk, that was magnified
By its own reflection in the tide.

Meanwhile, his friend, through alley and
          street,
Wanders and watches with eager ears,
Till in the silence around him he hears
The muster of men at the barrack door,
The sound of arms, and the tramp of feet,
And the measured tread of the grenadiers,
Marching down to their boats on the shore.

Then he climbed the tower of the Old North
    Church,
By the wooden stairs, with stealthy tread,
To the belfry-chamber overhead,
And startled the pigeons from their perch
On the sombre rafters, that round him made
Masses and moving shapes of shade, —
By the trembling ladder, steep and tall,
To the highest window in the wall,
Where he paused to listen and look down
A moment on the roofs of the town,
And the moonlight flowing over all.

Beneath, in the churchyard, lay the dead,
In their night-encampment on the hill,
Wrapped in silence so deep and still
That he could hear, like a sentinel's tread,
The watchful night-wind, as it went
Creeping along from tent to tent,
And seeming to whisper: "All is well!"
A moment only he feels the spell
Of the place and the hour, and the secret
    dread
Of the lonely belfry and the dead;
For suddenly all his thoughts are bent
On a shadowy something far away,
Where the river widens to meet the bay, —
A line of black that bends and floats
On the rising tide, like a bridge of boats.

Meanwhile, impatient to mount and ride,
Booted and spurred, with a heavy stride
On the opposite shore walked Paul Revere.
Now he patted his horse's side,
Now gazed at the landscape far and near,
Then, impetuous, stamped the earth,
And turned and tightened his saddle-girth;
But mostly he watched with eager search
The belfry-tower of the Old North Church,
As it rose above the graves on the hill,
Lonely and spectral and sombre and still.
And lo! as he looks, on the belfry's height
A glimmer, and then a gleam of light!
He springs to the saddle, the bridle he
    turns,
But lingers and gazes, till full on his sight,
A second lamp in the belfry burns!

A hurry of hoofs in a village street,
A shape in the moonlight, a bulk in the dark,
And beneath, from the pebbles, in passing, a
    spark
Struck out by a steed flying fearless and fleet:
That was all! And yet, through the gloom
    and the light,
The fate of a nation was riding that night;
And the spark struck out by that steed, in his
    flight,
Kindled the land into flame with its heat.

He has left the village and mounted the steep,
And beneath him, tranquil and broad and
    deep,
Is the Mystic, meeting the ocean tides;
And under the alders that skirt its edge,
Now soft on the sand, now loud on the ledge,
Is heard the tramp of his steed as he rides.

It was twelve by the village clock,
When he crossed the bridge into Medford
    town.
He heard the crowing of the cock,
And the barking of the farmer's dog,
And felt the damp of the river fog,
That rises after the sun goes down.

It was one by the village clock,
When he galloped into Lexington.
He saw the gilded weathercock
Swim in the moonlight as he passed,
And the meeting-house windows, blank and
    bare,
Gaze at him with a spectral glare,
As if they already stood aghast
At the bloody work they would look upon.

It was two by the village clock,
When he came to the bridge in Concord town.
He heard the bleating of the flock,

And the twitter of birds among the trees,
And felt the breath of the morning breeze
Blowing over the meadows brown.
And one was safe and asleep in his bed
Who at the bridge would be first to fall,
Who that day would be lying dead,
Pierced by a British musket-ball.

You know the rest. In the books you have
          read,
How the British Regulars fired and fled, —
How the farmers gave them ball for ball,
From behind each fence and farm-yard wall,
Chasing the red-coats down the lane,
Then crossing the fields to emerge again
Under the trees at the turn of the road,
And only pausing to fire and load.

So through the night rode Paul Revere;
And so through the night went his cry of
          alarm
To every Middlesex village and farm, —
A cry of defiance and not of fear,
A voice in the darkness, a knock at the door,
And a word that shall echo forevermore!
For, borne on the night-wind of the Past,
Through all our history, to the last,
In the hour of darkness and peril and need,
The people will waken and listen to hear

The hurrying hoof-beats of that steed
And the midnight message of Paul Revere.

Henry Wadsworth Longfellow.

REUBEN JAMES

(*August 3, 1804*)

THREE ships of war had Preble when he left
    the Naples shore,
And the knightly King of Naples lent him seven
    galleys more,
And never since the Argo floated in the middle
    sea
Such noble men and valiant have sailed in
    company
As the men who went with Preble to the siege
    of Tripoli.
Stewart, Bainbridge, Hull, Decatur — how
    their names ring out like gold!
Lawrence, Porter, Trippe, Macdonough, and
    a score as true and bold;
Every star that lights their banner tells the
    glory that they won;
But one common sailor's glory is the splendor
    of the sun.

Reuben James was first to follow when Deca-
    tur laid aboard
Of the lofty Turkish galley and in battle
    broke his sword.

Then the pirate captain smote him, till his
    blood was running fast,
And they grappled and they struggled, and
    they fell beside the mast.
Close behind him Reuben battled with a
    dozen, undismayed,
Till a bullet broke his sword-arm, and he
    dropped the useless blade.
Then a swinging Turkish sabre clove his left
    and brought him low,
Like a gallant bark, dismasted, at the mercy
    of the foe.
Little mercy knows the corsair: high his blade
    was raised to slay,
When a richer prize allured him where Decatur
    struggling lay.
"Help!" the Turkish leader shouted, and his
    trusty comrade sprung,
And his scimitar like lightning o'er the
    Yankee captain swung.

Reuben James, disabled, armless, saw the
    sabre flashed on high,
Saw Decatur shrink before it, heard the
    pirate's taunting cry,
Saw, in half the time I tell it, how a sailor
    brave and true
Still might show a bloody pirate what a dying
    man can do.

Quick he struggled, stumbling, sliding in the
  blood around his feet,
As the Turk a moment waited to make ven-
  geance doubly sweet.
Swift the sabre fell, but swifter bent the sail-
  or's head below,
And upon his 'fenceless forehead Reuben
  · James received the blow!

So was saved our brave Decatur; so the com-
  mon sailor died;
So the love that moves the lowly lifts the
  great to fame and pride.
Yet we grudge him not his honors, for whom
  love like this had birth —
For God never ranks His sailors by the Regis-
  ter of earth!

James Jeffrey Roche.

SACRED STORIES AND LEGENDS

THE THREE KINGS OF COLOGNE

From out Cologne there came three kings
  To worship Jesus Christ, their King.
To Him they sought fine herbs they brought,
  And many a beauteous golden thing;
They brought their gifts to Bethlehem town,
And in that manger set them down.

Then spake the first king, and he said:
  "O Child, most heavenly, bright, and fair!
I bring this crown to Bethlehem town,
  For Thee, and only Thee, to wear;
So give a heavenly crown to me,
When I shall come at last to Thee!"

The second, then. "I bring Thee here
  This royal robe, O Child!" he cried;
"Of silk 't is spun, and such an one
  There is not in the world beside;
So in the day of doom requite
Me with a heavenly robe of white!"

The third king gave his gift, and quoth:
  "Spikenard and myrrh to Thee I bring,
And with these twain would I most fain
  Anoint the body of my King;

So may their incense sometimes rise
To plead for me in yonder skies!"

Thus spake the three kings of Cologne,
  That gave their gifts, and went their way;
And now kneel I in prayer hard by
  The cradle of the Child to-day;
Nor crown, nor robe, nor spice I bring
As offering unto Christ, my King.

Yet have I brought a gift the Child
  May not despise, however small;
For here I lay my heart to-day
  And it is full of love to all.
Take Thou the poor but loyal thing,
My only tribute, Christ, my King!

Eugene Field.

BABOUSCKA

A Russian Legend of Christmas

BABOUSCKA sits before the fire,
  Upon a winter's night,
The driving winds heap up the snow,
  Her hut is snug and tight;
The howling winds, they only make
  Babouscka's fire more bright!

She hears a knocking at the door,
  So late — who can it be?

THE THREE KINGS

She hastes to lift the wooden latch
  (No thought of fear has she):
The wind-blown candle in her hand
  Shines out on strangers three.

Their beards are white with age, and snow
  That in the darkness flies;
Their floating locks are long and white,
  But kindly are the eyes
That sparkle underneath their brows,
  Like stars in frosty skies.

"Babouscka, we have come from far;
  We tarry but to say,
A little Prince is born this night
  Who all the world shall sway.
Come join the search; come, go with us
  Who go these gifts to pay."

Babouscka shivers at the door:
  "I would I might behold
The little Prince who shall be King;
  But ah, the night is cold,
The wind so fierce, the snow so deep,
  And I, good sirs, am old!"

The strangers three, no word they speak,
  But fade in snowy space —
Babouscka sits before the fire,
  And looks with wistful face:

"I wish that I had questioned them,
  So I the way might trace!

"When morning comes, with blessed light,
  I 'll early be awake.
My staff in hand, I 'll go — perchance,
  Those strangers overtake.
And for the Child, some little toys
  I 'll carry for His sake."

The morning came, and, staff in hand,
  She wandered in the snow;
And asked the way of all she met,
  But none the way could show.
"It must be farther yet," she sighed,
  "Then farther will I go."

And still 't is said, on Christmas eve,
  When high the drifts are piled,
With staff, and basket on her arm,
  Babouscka seeks the Child.
At every door her face is seen —
  Her wistful face and mild!

At every door her gifts she leaves,
  And bends, and murmurs low,
Above each little face half hid
  By pillows white as snow:
"And is *He* here?" — then softly sighs:
  "Nay; farther must I go!"

Edith M. Thomas.

THE PARABLE OF ST. CHRISTOPHER

From The Golden Legend

To a king's court a Giant came, —
  "O King, both far and near
I seek," he said, "the Greatest King;
  And thou art he, I hear.

"If it please thee, I will abide;
  To thee my knee shall bend;
Only unto *the Greatest Kings*
  Can giants condescend."

Right glad the King the Giant took
  Into his service then,
For since Goliath's mighty days
  No man so big was seen.

Well pleased the Giant, too, to serve
  The Greatest King on earth;
He served him well, in peace, in war,
  In sorrow, and in mirth,

Till came a wandering minstrel by,
  One day, who played and sang
Wild songs, through which the devil's name
  Profanely, loudly rang.

Astonished then the Giant saw
  The King look sore afraid;

At mention of the devil's name,
The cross's sign he made.

"How now, my master! Why dost thou
Make on thy breast this sign?"
He said. "It is a spell," replied
The King — "a spell divine,

"Which shall the devil circumvent,
And keep me safe and whole
From all the wicked arts he tries
To slay my precious soul."

"Oh, ho, my master! then he is
More powerful than thou!
They lied who called thee Greatest King;
I leave thy service now,

"And seek the devil; him will I
My master call henceforth,"
The Giant cried, and strode away
Contemptuous and wroth.

He found the devil soon. I ween
The devil waited near,
Well pleased to have this mighty man
Within his ranks appear.

They journeyed on full many a day,
And now the Giant deemed

At last he had a master found,
  Who was the king he seemed.

But lo! one day they came apace
  To where four road-ways met,
And at the meeting of the roads
  A cross of stone was set.

The devil trembled and fell back,
  And said: "We go around."
"Now tell me," fierce the Giant cried,
  "Why fearest thou this ground?"

The devil would not answer. "Then
  I leave thee, master mine,"
The Giant said. "Of something wrong
  This mystery is sign."

Then answered him the fiend, ashamed:
  "'T was there Christ Jesus died;
Wherever stands a cross like that,
  I may not, dare not bide."

"Ho, ho!" the Giant cried again,
  Surprised again, perplexed;
"Then Jesus is the Greatest King, —
  I seek and serve him next."

The King named Jesus, far and near,
  The weary Giant sought;

His name was everywhere proclaimed,
    His image sold and bought,

His power vaunted, and his laws
    Upheld by sword and fire;
But him the Giant sought in vain,
    Until he cried in ire,

One winter eve, as late he came
    Upon a hermit's cell:
"Now by my troth, tell me, good saint,
    Where doth thy master dwell?

"For I have sought him far and wide,
    By leagues of land and sea;
I seek to be his servant true,
    In honest fealty.

"I have such strength as kings desire,
    State to their state to lend;
But only to the Greatest King
    Can giants condescend."

Then said the hermit, pale and wan:
    "Oh, giant man! indeed
The King thou seekest doth all kings
    In glorious power exceed;

"But they who see him face to face,
    In full communion clear,

Crowned with his kingdom's splendor bright,
  Must buy the vision dear.

"Dwell here, O brother, and thy lot
  With ours contented cast,
And first, that flesh be well subdued,
  For days and nights thou 'lt fast!"

"I fast!" the Giant cried, amazed.
  "Good saint, I 'll no such thing.
My strength would fail; without that, I
  Were fit to serve no king!"

"Then thou must pray," the hermit said;
  "We kneel on yonder stone,
And tell these beads, and for each bead
  A prayer, one by one."

The Giant flung the beads away,
  Laughing in scornful pride.
"I will not wear my knees on stones;
  I know no prayers," he cried.

Then said the hermit: "Giant, since
  Thou canst not fast nor pray,
I know not if our Master will
  Save thee some other way.

"But go down to yon river deep,
  Where pilgrims daily sink,

And build for thee a little hut
  Close on the river's brink,

"And carry travelers back and forth
  Across the raging stream;
Perchance this service to our King
  A worthy one will seem."

"Now that is good," the Giant cried;
  "That work I understand;
A joyous task 't will be to bear
  Poor souls from land to land,

"Who, but for me, would sink and drown.
  Good saint, thou hast at length
Made mention of a work which is
  Fit for a giant's strength."

For many a year, in lowly hut,
  The Giant dwelt content
Upon the bank, and back and forth
  Across the stream he went,

And on his giant shoulders bore
  All travelers who came,
By night, by day, or rich or poor,
  All in King Jesus' name.

But much he doubted if the King
  His work would note or know,

And often with a weary heart
  He waded to and fro.

One night, as wrapped in sleep he lay,
  He sudden heard a call:
"Oh, Christopher, come carry me!"
  He sprang, looked out, but all

Was dark and silent on the shore.
  "It must be that I dreamed,"
He said, and laid him down again;
  But instantly there seemed

Again the feeble, distant cry:
  "Oh, come and carry me!"
Again he sprang, and looked; again
  No living thing could see.

The third time came the plaintive voice,
  Like infant's soft and weak;
With lantern strode the Giant forth,
  More carefully to seek.

Down on the bank a little Child
  He found, — a piteous sight, —
Who, weeping, earnestly implored
  To cross that very night.

With gruff good-will, he picked him up,
  And on his neck to ride,

He tossed him, as men play with babes,
  And plunged into the tide.

But as the water closed around
  His knees, the Infant's weight
Grew heavier and heavier,
  Until it was so great

The Giant scarce could stand upright,
  His staff shook in his hand,
His mighty knees bent under him,
  He barely reached the land,

And, staggering, set the Infant down,
  And turned to scan his face;
When, lo! he saw a halo bright
  Which lit up all the place.

Then Christopher fell down afraid
  At marvel of the thing,
And dreamed not that it was the face
  Of Jesus Christ, his King,

Until the Infant spoke, and said:
  "Oh, Christopher, behold!
I am the Lord whom thou hast served!
  Rise up, be glad, and bold!

For I have seen and noted well
  Thy works of charity;

And that thou art my servant good,
　A token thou shalt see.

"Plant firmly here upon this bank
　Thy stalwart staff of pine,
And it shall blossom and bear fruit,
　This very hour, in sign."

Then, vanishing, the Infant smiled.
　The Giant, left alone,
Saw on the bank, with luscious dates
　His stout pine staff bent down.

For many a year, St. Christopher
　Served God in many a land;
And master painters drew his face,
　With loving heart and hand,

On altar fronts and church's walls;
　And peasants used to say,
To look on good St. Christopher
　Brought luck, for all the day.

I think the lesson is as good
　To-day as it was then —
As good to us called Christians
　As to the heathen men.

(Condensed.) Helen Hunt Jackson.

THE LEGEND OF EASTER EGGS

TRINITY bells with their hollow lungs,
And their vibrant lips and their brazen
   tongues,
Over the roofs of the city pour
Their Easter music with joyous roar,
Till the soaring notes to the Sun are rolled
As he swings along in his path of gold.

"Dearest Papa," says my boy to me,
As he merrily climbs on his mother's knee,
"Why are these eggs that you see me hold
Colored so finely with blue and gold?
And what is the wonderful bird that lays
Such beautiful eggs upon Easter days?"

Tenderly shine the April skies,
Like laughter and tears in my child's blue
   eyes,
And every face in the street is gay, —
Why cloud this youngster's by saying nay?
So I cudgel my brains for the tale he begs,
And tell him this story of Easter eggs: —

You have heard, my boy, of the Man who
   died,
Crowned with keen thorns and crucified;

And how Joseph the wealthy — whom God
    reward! —
Cared for the corse of his martyred Lord,
And piously tombed it within the rock,
And closed the gate with a mighty block.

Now, close by the tomb a fair tree grew,
With pendulous leaves and blossoms of blue;
And deep in the green tree's shadowy breast
A beautiful singing bird sat on her nest,
Which was bordered with mosses like mala-
    chite,
And held four eggs of an ivory white.

Now, when the bird from her dim recess
Beheld the Lord in His burial dress,
And looked on the heavenly face so pale,
And the dear hands pierced with the cruel
    nail,
Her heart nigh broke with a sudden pang,
And out of the depth of her sorrow she sang.

All night long till the moon was up
She sat and sang in her moss-wreathed cup;
A song of sorrow as wild and shrill
As the homeless wind when it roams the hill;
So full of tears, so loud and long,
That the grief of the world seemed turned to
    song.

But soon there came through the weeping
    night
A glittering Angel clothed in white;
And he rolled the stone from the tomb away,
Where the Lord of the earth and the heavens
    lay;
And Christ arose in the cavern's gloom,
And in living lustre came from the tomb.

Now, the bird that sat in the heart of the tree
Beheld this celestial mystery,
And its heart was filled with a sweet delight,
And it poured a song on the throbbing night, —
Notes climbing notes, till higher, higher,
They shot to Heaven like spears of fire.

When the glittering white-robed Angel heard
The sorrowing song of the grieving bird,
And, after, the jubilant pæan of mirth
That hailed Christ risen again on earth,
He said: "Sweet bird, be forever blest,
Thyself, thy eggs, and thy moss-wreathed
    nest!"

And ever, my child, since that blessèd night,
When Death bowed down to the Lord of
    Light,
The eggs of that sweet bird change their hue;
And burn with red and gold and blue:

Reminding mankind in their simple way
Of the holy marvel of Easter Day.

Fitz-James O'Brien.

GOOD KING WENCESLAS

Good King Wenceslas looked out
    On the Feast of Stephen,
When the snow lay round about,
    Deep, and crisp, and even.
Brightly shone the moon that night,
    Though the frost was cruel,
When a poor man came in sight,
    Gath'ring winter fuel.

"Hither, page, and stand by me,
    If thou know'st it, telling,
Yonder peasant, who is he?
    Where and what his dwelling?"
"Sire, he lives a good league hence,
    Underneath the mountain;
Right against the forest fence,
    By Saint Agnes' fountain."

"Bring me flesh, and bring me wine,
    Bring me pine-logs hither:
Thou and I will see him dine,
    When we bear them thither."

Page and monarch forth they went,
  Forth they went together;
Through the rude wind's wild lament
  And the bitter weather.

"Sire, the night is darker now,
  And the wind blows stronger;
Fails my heart, I know not how,
  I can go no longer."
"Mark my footsteps, good my page;
  Tread thou in them boldly:
Thou shalt find the winter's rage
  Freeze thy blood less coldly."

In his master's steps he trod,
  Where the snow lay dinted;
Heat was in the very sod
  Which the saint had printed.
Therefore, Christian men, be sure,
  Wealth or rank possessing,
Ye who now will bless the poor,
  Shall yourselves find blessing.

Old Carol.

BROTHER HUBERT

HOLY-THOUGHTED Brother Hubert,
  In his cell one evening sat,

Painting angels in a missal
  Which he long had labored at;

Till the ringers in the belfry
  Chimed the hour of setting sun,
And he closed his precious volume,
  Saying: "Now my work is done.

"Time flies fast when one paints angels;
  I had not thought it was so late;
I must go and feed the poor folk
  Waiting at the Convent gate."

Kneeling low, he prayed a moment,
  Turning then to leave the room,
Started — for he saw a figure
  Standing in a purple gloom.

Sharpest thorns his head surrounded,
  Cruel cords his thin wrists bound,
In his hands and feet were nail-prints,
  In his side a spear-point wound;

And a purely glowing radiance
  From his face was shed abroad;
By these signs the pious Hubert
  Knew the vision was his Lord.

On his Master, glory stricken,
  Long the Monk gazed silently,

Till the thought arose within him
"Ah! how blessèd I should be

"Could my eyes but dwell forever
On that dear, that glorious head;
But below the Convent children
Wait impatient to be fed."

Straightway where the poor folk waited
For their evening dole he went,
Since the monks, though worn by fasting,
For the needy kept no Lent.

And good Hubert every sunset,
(As the Convent book records),
At the gate stood giving freely
Bread and wine and loving words.

So this evening all the poor folk
Feasted to their hearts' content,
Till they left the gateway taking
Hubert's blessing as they went.

Swiftly then the good Monk hastened
Down the halls and through his door;
Lo! the vision still was waiting,
Only brighter than before.

And the Master, turning on him
Eyes of blessing, smiled and said:

"Feeding these ones thou hast fed me,
Hadst thou staid I must have fled."

From an Old Legend.

ST. FRANCIS' SERMON TO THE BIRDS

Around Assisi's convent gate
The birds, God's poor who cannot wait,
From moor and mere and darksome wood
Come flocking for their dole of food.

"O brother birds," St. Francis said,
"Ye come to me and ask for bread,
But not with bread alone to-day
Shall ye be fed and sent away.

"Ye shall be fed, ye happy birds,
With manna of celestial words;
Not mine, though mine they seem to be,
Not mine, though they be spoken through me.

"Oh, doubly are ye bound to praise
The great Creator in your lays;
He giveth you your plumes of down,
Your crimson hoods, your cloaks of brown.

"He giveth you your wings to fly
And breathe a purer air on high,

And careth for you everywhere,
Who for yourselves so little care!"

With flutter of swift wings and songs
Together rose the feathered throngs,
And singing scattered far apart;
Deep peace was in St. Francis' heart.

He knew not if the brotherhood
His homily had understood;
He only knew that to one ear
The meaning of his words was clear.

(*Condensed.*) *Henry Wadsworth Longfellow.*

THE ABBOT OF INISFALEN

I

THE Abbot of Inisfalen
  Awoke ere dawn of day;
Under the dewy green leaves
  Went he forth to pray.

The lake around his island
  Lay smooth and dark and deep,
And, wrapt in a misty stillness,
  The mountains were all asleep.

Low kneel'd the Abbot Cormac,
  When the dawn was dim and gray;

The prayers of his holy office
  He faithfully 'gan say.

Low kneel'd the Abbot Cormac,
  When the dawn was waxing red,
And for his sins' forgiveness
  A solemn prayer he said.

Low kneel'd that holy Abbot
  When the dawn was waxing clear;
And he pray'd with loving-kindness
  For his convent brethren dear.

Low kneel'd that blessed Abbot,
  When the dawn was waxing bright;
He pray'd a great prayer for Ireland,
  He pray'd with all his might.

Low kneel'd that good old father,
  While the sun began to dart;
He pray'd a prayer for all mankind,
  He pray'd it from his heart.

II

The Abbot of Inisfalen
  Arose upon his feet;
He heard a small bird singing,
  And, oh, but it sung sweet!

He heard a white bird singing well
  Within a holly-tree;
A song so sweet and happy
  Never before heard he.

It sung upon a hazel,
  It sung upon a thorn;
He had never heard such music
  Since the hour that he was born.

It sung upon a sycamore,
  It sung upon a briar;
To follow the song and hearken
  This Abbot could never tire.

Till at last he well bethought him
  He might no longer stay;
So he bless'd the little white singing-bird,
  And gladly went his way.

III

But when he came to his Abbey walls,
  He found a wondrous change;
He saw no friendly faces there,
  For every face was strange.

The strangers spoke unto him;
  And he heard from all and each

The foreign tone of the Sassenach,
  Not wholesome Irish speech.

Then the oldest monk came forward,
  In Irish tongue spake he:
"Thou wearest the holy Augustine's dress,
  And who hath given it to thee?"

"I wear the holy Augustine's dress,
  And Cormac is my name,
The Abbot of this good Abbey
  By grace of God I am.

"I went forth to pray, at the dawn of
      day;
  And when my prayers were said,
I hearkened awhile to a little bird
  That sung above my head."

The monks to him made answer,
  "Two hundred years have gone o'er,
Since our Abbot Cormac went through
      the gate,
  And never was heard of more.

"Matthias now is our Abbot,
  And twenty have passed away.
The stranger is lord of Ireland;
  We live in an evil day."

IV

"Now give me absolution;
   For my time is come," said he.
And they gave him absolution
   As speedily as might be.

Then, close outside the window,
   The sweetest song they heard
That ever yet since the world began
   Was uttered by any bird.

The monks looked out and saw the bird,
   Its feathers all white and clean;
And there in a moment, beside it,
   Another white bird was seen.

Those two they sang together,
   Waved their white wings, and fled;
Flew aloft, and vanished;
   But the good old man was dead.

They buried his blessed body
   Where lake and greensward meet;
A carven cross above his head,
   A holly-bush at his feet;

Where spreads the beautiful water
   To gay or cloudy skies,
And the purple peaks of Killarney
   From ancient woods arise.

William Allingham.

THE MONK OF HEISTERBACH

In cloister Heisterbach a youthful monk
Went sauntering through the garden's far-
    thest ground,
Reading God's Holy Word in silence, sunk
In musing on eternity profound.

He reads, and hears the Apostle Peter say:
"One day is with the Lord a thousand years,
A thousand years with him are but a day,"—
But, in his maze of doubt, no clew appears.

He heeds not, lost in thought, the flight of
    time,
And deeper in the wood is lost his track,
Until the bell, with holy vesper chime,
To serious cloister-duties calls him back.

He reaches with swift steps the gate; the hand
Of an unknown one answers now the bell;
He starts — but sees the church all lighted
    stand,
And hears the friars the holy chorus swell.

Then, entering, to his seat he straightway goes,
But strange to tell, he finds it occupied;
He looks upon the monks in their long rows,
He sees all strangers, there, on every side.

The staring one is stared at all around,
They ask his name, and why he there appears;
He tells, — low murmurs through the chapel
    sound!
"None such has lived here these three hun-
    dred years.

"The last who bore the name," out spake the
    crowd,
"A doubter was, and disappeared one day;
None, since, to take that name has been
    allowed" —
He hears the word, and shudders with dismay.

He names the abbot now, and names the year:
They call for the old cloister-book, and lo!
A mighty miracle of God is clear:
'T is he was lost three hundred years ago!

The terror palsies him,— his hair grows gray,—
A deathly paleness settles on his face, —
He sinks, — while breath enough is left to say:
"God is exalted over time and space!

"What he had hid, a miracle now clears;
Think of my fate, believe, adore, obey!
I know: a day is as a thousand years
With God, a thousand years are as a day!"

From the German of Karl Wilhelm Müller.
Translated by C. T. Brooks.

A LEGEND OF TOLEDO

FAR down below the Christian captives pine
  In dungeon depths, and whoso dares to
      bring
Assuagements for their wounds, or food, or
      wine,
  Must brave the fiercest vengeance of the
      King.

Richly is spread above the royal board,
  The palace windows blaze with festal light,
And many a lady, many a Moorish lord,
  The morning's triumph celebrate at night.

But could they all without remorse or fear
  Feast, as though on earth were to be found
No hunger to appease, no want to cheer,
  No dark and hopeless places underground?

Neither of knight nor captain is it told
  That he was shamed at heart to do this
      thing;
One only was there, pitiful and bold —
  A maiden, daughter of this impious King.

Three times the beauteous messenger of grace
  She, passing to the dungeon from the hall,

Shone like an angel in that gloomy place,
  And brought relief to some, and hope to all.

But envious eyes were on her, and her sire,
  Upon her way, encountering unawares
Her passing thither the fourth time, in ire
  Bids show what hidden in her lap she bears.

Thus, willing to condemn her in the sight
  Of all, he spake: she tremblingly obeyed,
When, if old legends speak the truth aright,
  Flowers filled her lap, — those only it dis-
    played:

Roses and pinks and lilies there were found,
  Marvel to her and them who saw the same;
All sweetest flowers that grow from earthly
    ground,
  But nothing that might bring rebuke or
    blame.

Whate'er is sown in love — the lowliest deed —
  Shall bloom and be a flower in Paradise;
Yet springs not often from that precious seed
  Harvest so prompt as this before our eyes.

But afterward how rescued from the court,
  And from a faith which cannot save or bless,
To far-off hermitage she made resort,
  A saintly dweller in the wilderness,

Her story, pictured on a cloister wall
  In old Toledo, gives us not to know:
This only there appears, and this is all
  We need to ask, whether of weal or woe —

That unto her who was in mercy bold,
  Was given the knowledge of a faith divine;
For there in death we see her, and her hold
  Is on the Cross, salvation's blessed sign.

Richard Chenevix Trench.

KING SOLOMON AND THE BEES

A Tale of the Talmud

WHEN Solomon was reigning in his glory,
  Unto his throne the Queen of Sheba came
(So in the Talmud you may read the story)
  Drawn by the magic of the monarch's fame,
To see the splendors of his court, and bring
Some fitting tribute to the mighty King.

Nor this alone: much had her Highness heard
  What flowers of learning graced the royal
    speech;
What gems of wisdom dropped with every
    word;
  What wholesome lessons he was wont to
    teach

In pleasing proverbs; and she wished, in
    sooth,
To know if Rumor spoke the simple truth.

Besides, the Queen had heard (which piqued
    her most)
  How through the deepest riddles he could
    spy;
How all the curious arts that women boast
  Were quite transparent to his piercing eye;
And so the Queen had come — a royal guest —
To put the sage's cunning to the test.

And straight she held before the monarch's
    view,
  In either hand, a radiant wreath of flowers;
The one, bedecked with every charming hue,
  Was newly culled from Nature's choicest
    bowers;
The other, no less fair in every part,
Was the rare product of divinest Art.

"Which is the true, and which the false?" she
    said.
  Great Solomon was silent. All-amazed,
Each wondering courtier shook his puzzled
    head;
  While at the garlands long the monarch
    gazed,

As one who sees a miracle, and fain
For very rapture, ne'er would speak again.

"Which is the true?" once more the woman
    asked,
  Pleased at the fond amazement of the King,
"So wise a head should not be hardly tasked,
  Most learned Liege, with such a trivial
    thing!"
But still the sage was silent; it was plain
A deepening doubt perplexed the royal brain.

While thus he pondered, presently he sees,
  Hard by the casement — so the story goes —
A little band of busy, bustling bees,
  Hunting for honey in a withered rose.
The monarch smiled, and raised his royal
    head;
"Open the window!" — that was all he said.

The window opened at the King's command;
  Within the room the eager insects flew,
And sought the flowers in Sheba's dexter hand!
  And so the King and all the courtiers knew
That wreath was Nature's; and the baffled
    Queen
Returned to tell the wonders she had seen.

(Condensed.) John G. Saxe.

BISMILLAH

FORTH from his tent the patriarch Abraham
    stept,
And lengthening shadows slowly past him
    crept.

For many days he scarce had broke his fast,
Lest some poor wanderer should come at last,

And, scanty comfort finding, go his way,
In doubt of God's great mercy day by day.

But deep contentment in his calm eyes shone
When he beheld, afar, a pilgrim lone,

Fare slowly toward him from the flaming west,
With weary steps betokening need of rest.

When that he came anear, straightway was
    seen
An aged man of grave and reverend mien.

"Guest of mine eyes, here let thy footsteps
    halt,"
The patriarch said, " and share my bread and
    salt."

Then calling to his kinsfolk, soon the board
Was laden richly with the patriarch's hoard.

And when around the fair repast they drew,
"Bismillah!"[1] said they all with reverence due;

Save only he for whom the feast was spread;
He bowed him gravely, but no word he said.

Then Abraham thus: "O Guest, is it not meet
To utter God's great name ere thou dost eat?"

The pilgrim answered, courteous but calm,
"Good friend, of those who worship fire I am."

Then Abraham rose, his brow with anger bent
And drove the aged Gheber from his tent.

That instant, swifter than a flashing sword,
Appeared and spake an Angel of the Lord.

In shining splendor wrapt, the bright one said:
"An hundred years upon this aged head

"God's mercy hath been lavished from on
          high,
In life and sun and rain. Dost thou deny

"What God withholds not from the meanest
          clod?"
The patriarch bowed in meekness. Great is
          God!
David L. Proudfitt.

[1] "In the name of God."

ABOU BEN ADHEM AND THE ANGEL

ABOU BEN ADHEM (may his tribe increase!)
Awoke one night from a deep dream of peace,
And saw, within the moonlight in his room,
Making it rich, and like a lily in bloom,
An Angel, writing in a book of gold:—
Exceeding peace had made Ben Adhem bold,
And to the Presence in the room he said:
"What writest thou?"—The Vision raised
     its head,
And, with a look made of all sweet accord,
Answered: "The names of those who love the
     Lord."
"And is mine one?" said Abou. "Nay, not
     so,"
Replied the Angel. Abou spoke more low,
But cheerly still, and said:"I pray thee, then,
Write me as one that loves his fellow men."

The Angel wrote, and vanished. The next
     night
It came again with a great wakening light,
And showed the names whom love of God
     had blessed,
And, lo! Ben Adhem's name led all the rest.

Leigh Hunt.

THE BURIAL OF MOSES

"And He buried him in a valley in the land of Moab,
over against Beth-peor: but no man knoweth of his sepul-
chre unto this day."—Deut. xxxiv, 6.

By Nebo's lonely mountain,
  On this side Jordan's wave,
In a vale in the land of Moab,
  There lies a lonely grave.
And no man knows that sepulchre,
  And no man saw it e'er,
For the angels of God upturn'd the sod,
  And laid the dead man there.

That was the grandest funeral
  That ever passed on earth;
But no man heard the trampling,
  Or saw the train go forth, —
Noiselessly as the daylight
  Comes back when night is done,
And the crimson streak on ocean's cheek
  Grows into the great sun; —

Noiselessly as the spring-time
  Her crown of verdure weaves,
And all the trees on all the hills,
  Open their thousand leaves;
So without sound of music,
  Or voice of them that wept,

Silently down from the mountain's crown,
  The great procession swept.

Perchance the bald old eagle
  On grey Beth-peor's height,
Out of his lonely eyrie,
  Look'd on the wondrous sight;
Perchance the lion stalking
  Still shuns that hallow'd spot;
For beast and bird have seen and heard
  That which man knoweth not.

But when the warrior dieth,
  His comrades in the war,
With arms reversed and muffled drum,
  Follow his funeral car;
They show the banners taken,
  They tell his battles won,
And after him lead his masterless steed,
  While peals the minute-gun.

Amid the noblest of the land
  We lay the sage to rest,
And give the bard an honoured place,
  With costly marble drest,
In the great minster transept
  Where lights like glories fall,
And the organ rings, and the sweet choir sings
  Along the emblazoned wall.

This was the truest warrior
　　That ever buckled sword;
This the most gifted poet
　　That ever breathed a word;
And never earth's philosopher
　　Traced with his golden pen,
On the deathless page, truths half so sage
　　As he wrote down for men.

And had he not high honour —
　　The hill-side for a pall,
To lie in state, while angels wait
　　With stars for tapers tall,
And the dark rock-pines, like tossing plumes,
　　Over his bier to wave,
And God's own hand in that lonely land
　　To lay him in the grave?

In that strange grave without a name,
　　Whence his uncoffin'd clay
Shall break again, O wondrous thought!
　　Before the Judgment Day,
And stand with glory wrapt around
　　On the hills he never trod,
And speak of the strife, that won our life,
　　With the Incarnate Son of God.

O lonely grave in Moab's land!
　　O dark Beth-peor's hill!

Speak to these curious hearts of ours,
  And teach them to be still.
God hath his mysteries of grace,
  Ways that we cannot tell;
He hides them deep, like the hidden sleep
  Of him he loved so well.

Cecil Frances Alexander.

THE MIGHTY THREE

WATCHFIRES are blazing on hill and plain;
The noonday light is restored again;
There are shining arms in Raphaim's vale,
And bright is the glitter of clanging mail.

The Philistine hath fixed his encampment
    here;
Afar stretch his lines of banner and spear,
And his chariots of brass are ranged side by
    side,
And his war steeds neigh loud in their trap-
    pings of pride.

His tents are placed where the waters
    flow;
The sun hath dried up the springs below,
And Israel hath neither well nor pool,
The rage of her soldier's thirst to cool.

In the cave of Adullam King David lies,
Overcome with the glare of the burning skies;
And his lip is parched and his tongue is dry,
But none can the grateful draught supply.

Though a crownèd king, in that painful hour
One flowing cup might have bought his power.
What worth, in the fire of thirst, could be
The purple pomp of his sovereignty?

But no cooling cup from river or spring
To relieve his want can his servants bring;
And he cries: "Are there none in my train or
     state
Will fetch me the water of Bethlehem gate?"

Then three of his warriors, the "Mighty
     Three,"
The boast of the monarch's chivalry,
Uprose in their strength, and their bucklers
     rang,
As with eyes of flame on their steeds they
     sprang.

On their steeds they sprang, and with spurs of
     speed
Rushed forth in the strength of a noble deed,
And dashed on the foe like the torrent flood,
Till he floated away in a tide of blood.

To the right — to the left — where their blue
    swords shine,
Like autumn corn falls the Philistine;
And sweeping along with the vengeance of fate,
The "mighty" rush onward to Bethlehem
    gate.

Through a bloody gap in the shattered array,
To Bethlehem's gate they have hewn their
    way;
Then backward they turn on the corse-covered
    plain,
And charge through the foe to their monarch
    again.

The King looks at the cup, but the crystal
    draught
At a price too high for his want hath been
    bought;
They urge him to drink, but he wets not his
    lip
Though great is his need, he refuses to sip.

But he pours it forth to Heaven's Majesty,
He pours it forth to the Lord of the sky;
'T is a draught of death — 't is a cup blood-
    stained —
'T is a prize from man's suffering and agony
    gained.

Should he taste of a cup that his "Mighty
    Three"
Had obtained by their peril and jeopardy?
Should he drink of their life? 'T was the
    thought of a King;
And again he returned to his suffering.

Anonymous.

THE VISION OF BELSHAZZAR

THE King was on his throne,
    The Satraps thronged the hall;
A thousand bright lamps shone
    O'er that high festival.
A thousand cups of gold,
    In Judah deemed divine —
Jehovah's vessels hold
    The godless Heathen's wine.

In that same hour and hall,
    The fingers of a hand
Came forth against the wall,
    And wrote as if on sand:
The fingers of a man —
    A solitary hand
Along the letters ran,
    And traced them like a wand.

The monarch saw, and shook,
  And bade no more rejoice;
All bloodless waxed his look,
  And tremulous his voice.
"Let the men of lore appear,
  The wisest of the earth,
And expound the words of fear,
  Which mar our royal mirth."

Chaldea's seers are good,
  But here they have no skill;
And the unknown letters stood
  Untold and awful still.
And Babel's men of age
  Are wise and deep in lore;
But now they were not sage,
  They saw — but knew no more.

A captive in the land,
  A stranger and a youth,
He heard the King's command,
  He saw that writing's truth.
The lamps around were bright,
  The prophecy in view;
He read it on that night —
  The morrow proved it true.

"Belshazzar's grave is made,
  His kingdom passed away,

He, in the balance weighed,
Is light and worthless clay;
The shroud, his robe of state,
His canopy the stone;
The Mede is at his gate!
The Persian on his throne!"

George Gordon, Lord Byron.

THE DESTRUCTION OF SENNACHERIB

The Assyrian came down like the wolf on the fold,
And his cohorts were gleaming in purple and gold;
And the sheen of their spears was like stars on the sea,
When the blue wave rolls nightly on deep Galilee.

Like the leaves of the forest when Summer is green,
That host with their banners at sunset were seen:
Like the leaves of the forest when Autumn hath blown,
That host on the morrow lay withered and strown.

Unless, before the setting of the sun,
Mine eyes behold the Uncreated One!"

The Rabbi led him to the open air.
The oriental sun, with furious glare,
Sent down its rays, like beams of molten
    gold.
The aged teacher, pointing, said: "Behold."
"I cannot," said the prince. "My dazzled
    eyes
Refuse their service, turned upon the skies."

"Son of the dust," the Rabbi gently said,
And bowed with reverence his hoary head,
"This one creation thine eyes cannot be-
    hold,
Though by thy lofty state and pride made
    bold,
How canst thou, then, behold the God of
    Light,
Before whose face these sunbeams are as
    night?
Thine eyes, before this trifling labor fall,
Canst gaze on Him, who hath created all?
Son of the dust, repentance can atone;
Return and worship God, Who rules alone."

James Clarence Harvey.

KING ROBERT OF SICILY

Robert of Sicily, brother of Pope Urbane
And Valmond, Emperor of Allemaine,
Apparelled in magnificent attire,
With retinue of many a knight and squire,
On St. John's eve, at vespers, proudly sat
And heard the priests chant the Magnificat.
And as he listened, o'er and o'er again
Repeated, like a burden or refrain,
He caught the words, "*Deposuit potentes
De sede, et exaltavit humiles*";
And slowly lifting up his kingly head
He to a learned clerk beside him said:
"What mean these words?" The clerk made
    answer meet:
"He has put down the mighty from their seat,
And has exalted them of low degree."
Thereat King Robert muttered scornfully:
"'T is well that such seditious words are sung
Only by priests and in the Latin tongue;
For unto priests and people be it known,
There is no power can push me from my
    throne!"
And leaning back, he yawned and fell asleep,
Lulled by the chant monotonous and deep.
When he awoke, it was already night;
The church was empty, and there was no light,

Save where the lamps, that glimmered few
    and faint,
Lighted a little space before some saint.
He started from his seat and gazed around,
But saw no living thing and heard no sound.
He groped towards the door, but it was locked;
He cried aloud, and listened, and then
    knocked,
And uttered awful threatenings and com-
    plaints,
And imprecations upon men and saints.
The sounds reëchoed from the roof and walls
As if dead priests were laughing in their stalls.

At length the sexton, hearing from without
The tumult of the knocking and the shout,
And thinking thieves were in the house of
    prayer,
Came with his lantern, asking, "Who is there?"
Half choked with rage, King Robert fiercely
    said:
"Open: 't is I, the King! Art thou afraid?"
The frightened sexton, muttering, with a
    curse,
"This is some drunken vagabond, or worse!"
Turned the great key and flung the portal
    wide;
A man rushed by him at a single stride,
Haggard, half naked, without hat or cloak,

Who neither turned, nor looked at him, nor
          spoke,
But leaped into the blackness of the night,
And vanished like a spectre from his sight.

Robert of Sicily, brother of Pope Urbane
And Valmond, Emperor of Allemaine,
Despoiled of his magnificent attire,
Bareheaded, breathless, and besprent with
          mire,
With sense of wrong and outrage desperate,
Strode on and thundered at the palace gate;
Rushed through the courtyard, thrusting in
          his rage
To right and left each seneschal and page,
And hurried up the broad and sounding stair,
His white face ghastly in the torches' glare.
From hall to hall he passed with breathless
          speed;
Voices and cries he heard, but did not heed,
Until at last he reached the banquet-room,
Blazing with light, and breathing with per-
          fume.

There on the dais sat another king,
Wearing his robes, his crown, his signet-ring,
King Robert's self in features, form, and
          height,
But all transfigured with angelic light!

It was an Angel; and his presence there
With a divine effulgence filled the air,
An exaltation, piercing the disguise,
Though none the hidden Angel recognize.

A moment speechless, motionless, amazed,
The throneless monarch on the Angel gazed,
Who met his look of anger and surprise
With the divine compassion of his eyes;
Then said: "Who art thou? and why com'st
    thou here?"
To which King Robert answered with a sneer:
"I am the King, and come to claim my own
From an impostor, who usurps my throne!"
And suddenly, at these audacious words,
Up sprang the angry guests, and drew their
    swords;
The Angel answered, with unruffled brow:
"Nay, not the King, but the King's Jester, thou
Henceforth shalt wear the bells and scalloped
    cape,
And for thy counsellor shalt lead an ape;
Thou shalt obey my servants when they call,
And wait upon my henchmen in the hall!"

Deaf to King Robert's threats and cries and
    prayers,
They thrust him from the hall and down the
    stairs;

A group of tittering pages ran before,
And as they opened wide the folding-door,
His heart failed, for he heard, with strange
     alarms,
The boisterous laughter of the men-at-arms,
And all the vaulted chamber roar and ring
With the mock plaudits of "Long live the
     King!"

Next morning, waking with the day's first
     beam,
He said within himself: "It was a dream!"
But the straw rustled as he turned his head,
There were the cap and bells beside his bed,
Around him rose the bare, discolored walls,
Close by, the steeds were champing in their
     stalls,
And in the corner, a revolting shape,
Shivering and chattering sat the wretched
     ape.
It was no dream; the world he loved so much
Had turned to dust and ashes at his touch!
Days came and went; and now returned again
To Sicily the old Saturnian reign;
Under the Angel's governance benign
The happy island danced with corn and wine,
And deep within the mountain's burning
     breast
Enceladus, the giant, was at rest.

Meanwhile King Robert yielded to his fate,
Sullen and silent and disconsolate.
Dressed in the motley garb that Jesters wear,
With look bewildered and a vacant stare,
Close shaven above the ears, as monks are
    shorn,
By courtiers mocked, by pages laughed to
    scorn,
His only friend the ape, his only food
What others left, — he still was unsubdued.
And when the Angel met him on his way,
And half in earnest, half in jest, would say,
Sternly, though tenderly, that he might feel
The velvet scabbard held a sword of steel:
"Art thou the King?" the passion of his woe
Burst from him in resistless overflow,
And, lifting high his forehead, he would fling
The haughty answer back: "I am, I am the
    King!"

Almost three years were ended; when there
    came
Ambassadors of great repute and name
From Valmond, Emperor of Allemaine,
Unto King Robert, saying that Pope Urbane
By letter summoned them forthwith to come
On Holy Thursday to his city of Rome.
The Angel with great joy received his guests,
And gave them presents of embroidered vests,

And velvet mantles with rich ermine lined,
And rings and jewels of the rarest kind.
Then he departed with them o'er the sea
Into the lovely land of Italy,
Whose loveliness was more resplendent made
By the mere passing of that cavalcade,
With plumes, and cloaks, and housings, and the stir
Of jewelled bridle and of golden spur.
And lo! among the menials, in mock state,
Upon a piebald steed, with shambling gait,
His cloak of fox-tails flapping in the wind,
The solemn ape demurely perched behind,
King Robert rode, making huge merriment
In all the country towns through which they went.

The Pope received them with great pomp and blare
Of bannered trumpets, on Saint Peter's square,
Giving his benediction and embrace,
Fervent, and full of apostolic grace.
While with congratulations and with prayers
He entertained the Angel unawares,
Robert, the Jester, bursting through the crowd,
Into their presence rushed, and cried aloud:
"I am the King! Look, and behold in me
Robert, your brother, King of Sicily!
This man, who wears my semblance to your eyes,

Is an impostor in a king's disguise.
Do you not know me? does no voice within
Answer my cry, and say we are akin?"
The Pope in silence, but with troubled mien,
Gazed at the Angel's countenance serene;
The Emperor, laughing, said: "It is strange
     sport
To keep a madman for thy Fool at court!"
And the poor, baffled Jester in disgrace
Was hustled back among the populace.

In solemn state the Holy Week went by,
And Easter Sunday gleamed upon the sky;
The presence of the Angel, with its light,
Before the sun rose, made the city bright,
And with new fervor filled the hearts of men,
Who felt that Christ indeed had risen again.
Even the Jester, on his bed of straw,
With haggard eyes the unwonted splendor
     saw,
He felt within a power unfelt before,
And, kneeling humbly on his chamber floor,
He heard the rushing garments of the Lord
Sweep through the silent air, ascending heav-
     enward.

And now the visit ending, and once more
Valmond returning to the Danube's shore,
Homeward the Angel journeyed, and again

The land was made resplendent with his train,
Flashing along the towns of Italy
Unto Salerno, and from thence by sea.
And when once more within Palermo's wall,
And, seated on the throne in his great hall,
He heard the Angelus from convent towers,
As if the better world conversed with ours,
He beckoned to King Robert to draw nigher,
And with a gesture bade the rest retire;
And when they were alone, the Angel said:
"Art thou the King?" Then, bowing down his
        head,
King Robert crossed both hands upon his
        breast,
And meekly answered him: "Thou knowest
        best!
My sins as scarlet are; let me go hence,
And in some cloister's school of penitence,
Across those stones, that pave the way to
        heaven,
Walk barefoot, till my guilty soul be shriven!"

The Angel smiled, and from his radiant face
A holy light illumined all the place,
And through the open window, loud and clear,
They heard the monks chant in the chapel
        near,
Above the stir and tumult of the street:
"He has put down the mighty from their seat,

And has exalted them of low degree!"
And through the chant a second melody
Rose like the throbbing of a single string:
"I am an Angel, and thou art the King!"

King Robert, who was standing near the
    throne,
Lifted his eyes, and lo! he was alone!
But all apparelled as in days of old,
With ermined mantle and with cloth of gold;
And when his courtiers came, they found him
    there
Kneeling upon the floor, absorbed in silent
    prayer.

Henry Wadsworth Longfellow.

FRIAR JEROME'S BEAUTIFUL BOOK

(A.D. 1200)

THE FRIAR JEROME, for some slight sin,
Done in his youth, was struck with woe.
"When I am dead," quoth Friar Jerome,
"Surely, I think my soul will go
Shuddering through the darkened spheres,
Down to eternal fires below!
I shall not dare from that dread place
To lift mine eyes to Jesus' face,
Nor Mary's, as she sits adored

At the feet of Christ the Lord.
Alas! December 's all too brief
For me to hope to wipe away
The memory of my sinful May!"
And Friar Jerome was full of grief,
That April evening, as he lay
On the straw pallet in his cell.
He scarcely heard the curfew-bell
Calling the brotherhood to prayer;
But he arose, for 't was his care
Nightly to feed the hungry poor
That crowded to the Convent door.

His choicest duty it had been:
But this one night it weighed him down.
"What work for an immortal soul,
To feed and clothe some lazy clown!
Is there no action worth my mood,
No deed of daring, high and pure,
That shall, when I am dead, endure,
A well-spring of perpetual good?"

And straight he thought of those great tomes
With clamps of gold,—the Convent's boast,—
How they endured, while kings and realms
Past into darkness and were lost;
How they had stood from age to age,
Clad in their yellow vellum-mail,

'Gainst which the Paynim's godless rage,
The Vandal's fire, could naught avail:
Though heathen sword-blows fell like hail,
Though cities ran with Christian blood,
Imperishable they had stood!
They did not seem like books to him,
But Heroes, Martyrs, Saints, — themselves
The things they told of, not mere books
Ranged grimly on the oaken shelves.

To those dim alcoves, far withdrawn,
He turned with measured steps and slow,
Trimming his lantern as he went;
And there, among the shadows, bent
Above one ponderous folio,
With whose miraculous text were blent
Seraphic faces: Angels, crowned
With rings of melting amethyst;
Mute, patient Martyrs, cruelly bound
To blazing fagots; here and there,
Some bold, serene Evangelist,
Or Mary in her sunny hair:
And here and there from out the words
A brilliant tropic bird took flight;
And through the margins many a vine
Went wandering, — roses, red and white,
Tulip, wind-flower, and columbine
Blossomed. To his believing mind
These things were real, and the wind,

Blown through the mullioned window, took
Scent from the lilies in the book.

"Santa Maria!" cried Friar Jerome,
"Whatever man illumined this,
Though he were steeped heart-deep in sin,
Was worthy of unending bliss,
And no doubt hath it! Ah! dear Lord,
Might I so beautify Thy Word!
What sacristan, the convents through,
Transcribes with such precision? who
Does such initials as I do?
Lo! I will gird me to this work,
And save me, ere the one chance slips.
On smooth, clean parchment I'll engross
The Prophet's fell Apocalypse;
And as I write from day to day,
Perchance my sins will pass away."

So Friar Jerome began his Book.
From break of dawn till curfew-chime
He bent above the lengthening page,
Like some rapt poet o'er his rhyme.
He scarcely paused to tell his beads,
Except at night; and then he lay
And tost, unrestful, on the straw,
Impatient for the coming day, —
Working like one who feels, perchance,
That, ere the longed-for goal be won,

Ere beauty bare her perfect breast,
Black Death may pluck him from the sun.
At intervals the busy brook,
Turning the mill-wheel, caught his ear;
And through the grating of the cell
He saw the honeysuckles peer;
And knew 't was summer, that the sheep
In fragrant pastures lay asleep;
And felt, that, somehow, God was near.
In his green pulpit on the elm,
The robin, abbot of that wood,
Held forth by times; and Friar Jerome
Listened, and smiled, and understood.

While summer wrapt the blissful land,
What joy it was to labor so,
To see the long-tressed Angels grow
Beneath the cunning of his hand,
Vignette and tail-piece deftly wrought!
And little recked he of the poor
That missed him at the Convent door;
Or, thinking of them, put the thought
Aside. "I feed the souls of men
Henceforth, and not their bodies!" — yet
Their sharp, pinched features, now and then,
Stole in between him and his Book,
And filled him with a vague regret.

Now on that region fell a blight:
The corn grew cankered in its sheath;

And from the verdurous uplands rolled
A sultry vapor fraught with death, —
A poisonous mist, that, like a pall,
Hung black and stagnant over all.
Then came the sickness, — the malign
Green-spotted terror, called the Pest,
That took the light from loving eyes,
And made the young bride's gentle breast
A fatal pillow. Ah! the woe,
The crime, the madness that befell!
In one short night that vale became
More foul than Dante's inmost hell.
Men curst their wives; and mothers left
Their nursing babes alone to die,
And wantoned, singing, through the streets,
With shameless brow and frenzied eye;
And senseless clowns, not fearing God, —
Such power the spotted fever had, —
Razed Cragwood Castle on the hill,
Pillaged the wine-bins, and went mad.
And evermore that dreadful pall
Of mist hung stagnant over all:
By day, a sickly light broke through
The heated fog, on town and field;
By night the moon, in anger, turned
Against the earth its mottled shield.

Then from the Convent, two and two,
The Prior chanting at their head,

The monks went forth to shrive the sick,
And give the hungry grave its dead, —
Only Jerome, he went not forth,
But hiding in his dusty nook,
"Let come what will, I must illume
The last ten pages of my Book!"
He drew his stool before the desk,
And sat him down, distraught and wan,
To paint his darling masterpiece,
The stately figure of Saint John.
He sketched the head with pious care,
Laid in the tint, when, powers of Grace!
He found a grinning Death's-head there,
And not the grand Apostle's face!

Then up he rose with one long cry:
"'T is Satan's self does this," cried he,
"Because I shut and barred my heart
When Thou didst loudest call to me!
O Lord, Thou know'st the thoughts of men,
Thou know'st that I did yearn to make
Thy Word more lovely to the eyes
Of sinful souls, for Christ his sake!
Nathless, I leave the task undone:
I give up all to follow Thee, —
Even like him who gave his nets
To winds and waves by Galilee!"

Which said, he closed the precious Book
In silence with a reverent hand;

And, drawing his cowl about his face,
Went forth into the Stricken Land.
And there was joy in heaven that day, —
More joy o'er this forlorn old friar
Than over fifty sinless men
Who never struggled with desire!

What deeds he did in that dark town,
What hearts he soothed with anguish torn,
What weary ways of woe he trod,
Are written in the Book of God,
And shall be read at Judgment Morn.
The weeks crept on, when, one still day,
God's awful presence filled the sky,
And that black vapor floated by,
And, lo! the sickness past away.
With silvery clang, by thorpe and town,
The bells made merry in their spires,
Men kissed each other on the street,
And music piped to dancing feet
The livelong night, by roaring fires!

Then Friar Jerome, a wasted shape, —
For he had taken the Plague at last, —
Rose up, and through the happy town,
And through the wintry woodlands, past
Into the Convent. What a gloom
Sat brooding in each desolate room!
What silence in the corridor!

For of that long, innumerous train
Which issued forth a month before,
Scarce twenty had come back again!

Counting his rosary step by step,
With a forlorn and vacant air,
Like some unshriven churchyard thing,
The Friar crawled up the mouldy stair
To his damp cell, that he might look
Once more on his belovèd Book.

And there it lay upon the stand,
Open! — he had not left it so.
He grasped it, with a cry; for, lo!
He saw that some angelic hand,
While he was gone, had finished it!
There 't was complete, as he had planned!
There, at the end, stood FINIS, writ
And gilded as no man could do, —
Not even that pious anchoret,
Bilfrid, the wonderful, — nor yet
The miniatore Ethelwold, —
Nor Durham's Bishop, who of old
(England still hoards the priceless leaves)
Did the Four Gospels all in gold.
And Friar Jerome nor spoke nor stirred,
But, with his eyes fixed on that word,
He past from sin and want and scorn;
And suddenly the chapel bells
Rang in the holy Christmas-Morn!

In those wild wars which racked the land
Since then, and kingdoms rent in twain,
The Friar's Beautiful Book was lost, —
That miracle of hand and brain:
Yet, though its leaves were torn and tost,
The volume was not writ in vain!

Thomas Bailey Aldrich.

INDEXES

SUBJECT INDEX

Apple-Seed John, 46; Brier-Rose, 58; Opportunity, 71; Enchanted Shirt, 167; Quivira, 274; Reuben James, 292; Brother Hubert, 314; Friar Jerome's Beautiful Book, 354.

THANKSGIVING. First Thanksgiving Day, 281; St. Francis' Sermon to the Birds, 317; Bismillah, 330.

THRIFT. Ant and the Cricket, 3.

TREASURE STORIES. Good Man of Alloa, 30; Brown Dwarf of Rügen, 125; Nibelungen Treasure, 239.

TREES AND ARBOR DAY. Elm and the Vine, 40; Gourd and the Palm, 41; Plucky Prince, 41; Apple-Seed John, 46; Woodman and the Sandal Tree, 49; Brier-Rose, 58.

TRUTH-TELLING AND LYING. False Alarms, 7; Charley the Story-Teller, 9; Fairy Boy, 93; Pied Piper, 98.

VAIN-GLORY. Two Church-Builders, 77.

VANITY. Glove and the Lions, 69.

VISIONS AND ANGELS. Two Church-Builders, 77; Parable of St. Christopher, 301; Legend of Easter Eggs, 310; Brother Hubert, 314; Bismillah, 330; Abou Ben Adhem, 332; Vision of Belshazzar, 339; King Robert of Sicily, 345; Friar Jerome's Beautiful Book, 354.

WAR STORIES. Tubal Cain, 55; Opportunity, 71; Harmosan, 75; Faithless Nelly Gray, 186; Emperor's Bird's-Nest, 237; Battle of Blenheim, 243; Napoleon and the English Sailor Boy, 246; Incident of the French Camp, 249; King Alfred the Harper, 257; Taillefer the Minstrel, 263; Relief of Lucknow, 267; Reuben James, 292; Mighty Three, 336; Destruction of Sennacherib, 341.

WISDOM. King Solomon and the Bees, 327.

INDEX OF FIRST LINES

INDEX OF TITLES

INDEX OF AUTHORS